Charm C̶ [FAVORITES]

Famous Recipes from the Inn

The Charm

Countryview® Inn

Charm Countryview Inn, Inc.
Charm, Ohio

Additional copies of *Charm Countryview Favorites* may be obtained at the cost of $14.95 plus $3.00 postage and handling, each book. Ohio residents add $.97 sales tax, each book.

Send To:

Charm Countryview Inn
P.O. Box 100
Charm, Ohio 44617
www.charmcountryviewinn.com

ISBN: 0-9637560-0-1
LCCN: 93-73319

Copyright © 1994
Charm Countryview Inn, Inc.
Charm, Ohio

First Printing   10,000 copies   April 1994

Second Printing   1,250 copies   September 2005

Carlisle Printing
OF WALNUT CREEK Ltd.

INTRODUCTION

In the past few years since we have opened our Bed & Breakfast Inn our guests have often asked for many of our breakfast and also our evening snack recipes. We kept telling them we hoped to someday share these recipes with them in a cookbook. So, after many inquiries of, "Has your cookbook been completed yet?" we can finally say, "Yes!" We have included more than just breakfast and snack recipes though, and we hope you'll enjoy them all!

Although each of us has contributed some recipes, most of them come from Mom's collection that she has used over the years. Some recipes may be a little more complicated, but we believe you'll find that we appreciate quick and simple recipes as well!

We, as a family, would like to dedicate this book to all of our guests who have visited our Inn and who have enriched our lives by their friendship and love. We hope you will enjoy our cookbook and may God bless each one of you!

The 'Mast' Family

THE CHARM COUNTRYVIEW INN
Bed & Breakfast — Est. 1990

ACKNOWLEDGMENTS

A special thanks to Mom for sharing her recipes. This cookbook would not have been possible without her collection of recipes and years of experience.

Photography — Mark's Studio and Jim Smith

Artwork — Leon Ray Mast

Text — Dorothy & Marvin Raber

To Our Heavenly Father...

As we reflect on the Inn, dear God,
Our hearts are filled with praise
And gratitude for all You've done
You've blessed us in so many ways.

We thank You for the love of a family
And the work You have given us to do.
For health and strength and abilities
We know it all comes from You.

Thank you for those who work here
Keeping things clean and neat
We pray You would richly bless them
Each day as they dust and sweep.

We've been blessed by the people who've come
To our Inn, in these past several years
Those who once were only strangers to us
Are now among friends most dear!

We thank You for bringing them into our lives
It seems our family just keeps growing bigger!
We treasure the memories of warm, happy times
We've had, visiting and sharing together.

So help us, dear God, to be a blessing to all
Showing hospitality, kindness and love
For all that we have we owe to You, Lord
You have blessed us more than we're worthy of.

We thank You for giving Your Son Jesus
That whosoever believeth in Him
Should not perish but have life eternal
This promise to all You have given.

And so when our work here is done
And You call us to our home in the sky
May we all meet there as a big "family"
In Heaven where there'll be no more good-byes!

D. Raber

ABOUT THE INN

The Charm Countryview Inn, a bed and breakfast Inn, is located 2¹/₂ miles southeast of the small village of Charm, Ohio. The Inn perches on a quiet hillside overlooking peaceful country meadows and farms in Ohio's scenic Holmes County, home of the world's largest Amish Community. The Inn is owned and operated by us, the Abe Mast Family.

A Bed and Breakfast operation had been a dream of our family for several years. It seemed whenever we'd get together, the conversation would eventually come back to this idea of a B & B! The men especially often talked about this. In 1988 Leon and Marvin attended a B & B seminar and after that our family spent many evenings giving the idea careful thought.

There was never really a question about where the Inn would be built. Dad had bought a 70-acre farm in 1981 between Charm and Farmerstown and it had a perfect spot on a hill at the edge of the woods. So Leon began drawing up plans with much counsel from the rest of us. Our plans were then given to an architect who completed them and got the state approval required.

In the meantime we had to come up with a name for this new establishment. That turned out to be quite a challenge! Each of us came up with some names and when we put them all together we had around 50 different ones. Somehow we narrowed it down to one, *The Charm Countryview Inn*. We can't imagine it being anything different now.

The foundation for the Inn began in August of 1989, and the framework construction was completed in December. Our local carpenter crew worked all winter and spring until we opened the doors to our first guests on June 1, 1990.

Each of our 15 guest rooms, all with private baths, are individually decorated and have been named after members of our family. Our comfortably furnished rooms feature handmade quilts on queen size beds and solid oak furniture selected by Leon and Sara Ann from their furniture store.

We want our Inn to be a "destination." A place where people can come to unwind and relax, away from the hustle and bustle of life, and where you feel refreshed when you leave.

Reflecting back over the first few years of *The Charm Countryview Inn*, it really has been an exciting experience, made possible in part by the many feature articles in our local newspapers and also many prominent National Publications.

TABLE OF CONTENTS

Note: There are certain recipes in this book which call for clear jel. Clear jel is a cornstarch product that can be purchased at bulk food stores.

MEET OUR FAMILY...

Abe and Fannie Mast (referred to as Mom and Dad)...Dad grew up in a family of eight children. He lived in Wayne County, Ohio, during his childhood years. He and Mom were married on November 7, 1957. Since Mom was an only child she inherited her parents' home in Charm. They raised us five children there and we have many good memories of times spent together there at home as a family. Dad worked at Semac Industries, Inc. for 29 years and is now retired. Between helping at the Furniture Store and mowing lawn and washing dishes at the Inn, he stays busy though! We call Dad the "brains" of these businesses! If you should meet with Dad at the Inn or the Furniture Store you will find he loves to visit! Mom has always enjoyed cooking, baking and canning. She is always looking for new and different recipes to try on her family. She also likes gardening and always seems to plant more than she really needs! Her enjoyment of growing flowers shows up around the Inn during the summertime! The Inn has been the perfect place for her to exercise these talents.

Sara Ann...Sara Ann is the oldest in the family. She worked in the restaurant in Charm as a waitress for several years, then when Dad bought the feed mill right across the road from our home she became his secretary and sold feed! And now she still works at the "mill," only it's been turned into a furniture store, Ole Mill Furniture. So, she's gone from selling feed to furniture! She also enjoys cooking and baking but her decorating talent outshines all the rest! Sara Ann does most of the decorating at the Inn. The rest of us help but we usually get her approval first! She was married June 3, 1993, to Ivan Miller who is also a lifelong resident of Charm. He has a management position at Keim Lumber Co. there in town, where he has worked since he was 17. So whenever we have questions about anything from shingles to doorknobs we run to Ivan! He was in a bicycle accident at the age of 12 and broke his back. Although he is in a wheelchair, he is a very capable person and really enjoys life!

Naomi...Naomi is the second in line. She has always been a fun loving person and has what we call "the gift of gab!" As a teenager she worked at the General Store in Charm. She married Paul Miller on September 25, 1980. Paul grew up on a farm just north of Charm. He is the youngest of eight children. Paul and Naomi lived on the farm where the Inn was later built on during the first nine years of their marriage. Between farming, milking cows by hand and Paul working as a logger the two of them were kept busy during those years! Paul and Naomi are the parents of three children, Matthew Lee and a set of twins, Marcus Ryan and Maria Rose. Between the three of them they keep things quite lively! They, as a family, live at the Inn in their own private quarters, where they moved prior to the opening of the Inn, June 1, 1990. Naomi enjoys cooking and helping in the kitchen and with whatever needs to be done, while Paul, among other things, has become our bookkeeper and maintenance man. Innkeeping involves quite a variety of jobs as they have discovered! They have contributed much to the Inn by their friendly personality and gift of hospitality.

Leon Ray...Leon is the only boy in the family. He thinks he's had a rough life growing up with four sisters, but we think he's had it pretty nice! He used to also work in Dad's feed mill and is now co-owner of Ole Mill Furniture. Leon enjoys designing things—anything from furniture to landscaping and houses. In the very early stages of our plans for the Inn he drew up the look he wanted our Inn to have so our architect would have a better idea of what we had in mind. He seems to have a knack of picturing something in his mind and then has the ability of putting it on paper. It doesn't take much to keep him occupied, just a pencil and a piece of paper, and he'll sit down and draw for hours! He was married August 25, 1990, to Lois Mast, whose dad's name, incidentally, is also Abe Mast! She just fits right in and has really been a blessing. She enjoys cooking and used to be co-manager of a restaurant, so she has been put in charge of managing the Inn kitchen. Leon and Lois live in the farmhouse that belongs to the Inn farm.

Dorothy...That's me. I enjoy a lot of different things but probably at the top of the list is reading and writing. I got the job of helping with our brochure. I also like to sew and quilt and with the help of my mother-in-law made several quilts and wall hangings for the Inn. I used to work at the General Store in Charm until I met Marvin and became a farmer's wife! I married Marvin Raber on October 18, 1986. We live in the house he grew up in, on the family farm, about one mile out of Charm. Marvin took on his dad's business of boarding and raising horses. He likes to "dream" and the Inn is one of those "dreams" come true! When the rest of us felt like giving up, especially in those first stages of the building process when we found out about all the "red tape" involved, he was the one who never gave up but kept telling us all it wasn't as impossible as it looked and reassured us that it would be worth it! His hearty laugh and sense of humor keeps us from taking ourselves too seriously.

Carol...Last, but by far not least, is Carol. She is the youngest in the family and what we would do without her, I just don't know. She has kind of "grown up" along with the Inn and is capable of doing most anything that needs to be done. You may find her anywhere from taking reservations in the office and scrubbing the kitchen floor to doing laundry in the basement! She especially enjoys baking cookies for our evening snack that we serve at the Inn. Carol has often lightened up the day with her sense of humor! Her unlimited energy has been both a great help and an encouragement to all of us.

Much more could be said about what each one contributes to the Inn, and although there's a lot of work involved our guests make it all worthwhile!

Pictured on Reverse Side

Pancakes with Tropical Fruit Dessert
Walnut Wonder Coffee Cake with Creme Filling
Bran Muffins
Orange Muffins
Fruit Slush
Pluckets
and our Famous Fruit Pizza

Hash Browns
Pluckets
Scrambled Eggs
Cheese Sauce
Barbecued Ham Slices
Bran Muffins
Orange Muffins
Fruit Slush

OUR
BREAKFAST
SPECIALTIES

OUR BREAKFAST SPECIALTIES

Bacon, Egg and Cheese
Casserole 20
Baked Oatmeal 32
Barbequed Ham Slices 20
Barbequed Sausage................22
Blueberry Muffins 17
Bran Muffins 15
Breakfast Burritos...................21
Buttermilk Biscuits 19
Buttery Cinnamon Skillet
Apples 26
Cinnamon Banana Muffins......15
Creamy Coffee Cake Filling....30
Crunchy Crust French Toast...24
Easy Drop Biscuits 19
Family Cheese Sauce.............23
Finnish Coffee Cake 31
Fluffy Pancakes......................24
Fruit Pizza..............................25

Fruit Slush..............................26
Hash Browns 21
Homemade Granola Cereal 32
Lois' Cinnamon Rolls..............28
Mom's Cinnamon Rolls..........28
Nutty Baked French Toast......23
Orange Nut Muffins 16
Peaches 'n Cream Coffee
Cake 29
Pluckets.................................29
Pumpkin Apple Streusel
Muffins 17
Pumpkin Cinnamon Rolls 27
Raised Flapjacks 24
Rhubarb Muffins 18
Sausage Gravy 22
Tropical Fruit Dessert.............27
Walnut Wonder Coffee Cake ...30
Zucchini Muffins 18

BRAN MUFFINS

10 ounces raisin bran cereal
(4¹/₂ cups)
3 cups sugar
5 cups flour
2 teaspoons salt

5 teaspoons baking soda
4 beaten eggs
1 quart buttermilk
1 cup vegetable oil
1¹/₂ cups sour cream

Mix raisin bran, sugar, flour, salt and soda. Add eggs, sour cream, buttermilk and oil. Mix well. Put in a large bowl. Store, covered, in refrigerator for up to 6 weeks. When ready to bake put in greased muffin tins and bake at 350 degrees for 20-25 minutes. Do not stir when putting mix into muffin tins.

Yield: 50-60 muffins

CINNAMON BANANA MUFFINS

1 cup brown sugar, packed
2 ripe bananas, mashed
¹/₂ cup chopped nuts
1 cup margarine, divided
¹/₂ cup white sugar

2 eggs
1³/₄ cups flour
1 tablespoon cinnamon
1 teaspoon baking powder
1 teaspoon baking soda

GLAZE:
1¹/₄ cups powdered sugar

3 ounces cream cheese,
softened

In a small saucepan combine brown sugar with ¹/₂ cup margarine. Stir over medium heat until melted. Add bananas and nuts. Stir until well coated. Cool to room temperature. Cream remaining margarine and white sugar. Beat in eggs. Sift together flour, cinnamon, baking powder and baking soda. Add to creamed mixture. Stir in banana mixture. Fill greased muffin pans ²/₃ full. Bake at 350 degrees for 20-30 minutes. Cool. Combine powdered sugar and cream cheese and spread on muffins.

Yield: 1¹/₂ dozen

Learn by experience—preferably other people's.

ORANGE NUT MUFFINS

$^1/_4$ cup white sugar
$^1/_2$ cup brown sugar
$^1/_2$ cup margarine
1 egg
$2^1/_2$ cups flour
$2^1/_4$ teaspoons baking soda
$^3/_4$ teaspoon baking powder

$^1/_2$ teaspoon salt
1 cup sour cream
1 11 ounce can mandarin
   oranges
1 tablespoon orange extract
$^3/_4$ cup chopped walnuts

GLAZE:
2 cups powdered sugar
1 tablespoon vegetable oil

$^1/_4$ teaspoon vanilla
Hot water

Cream together sugars and margarine. Add egg. Sift together flour, soda, baking powder and salt. Add to creamed mixture alternately with sour cream. Drain oranges and reserve liquid. Cut oranges in half and place in an 8 ounce measuring cup. Add orange extract and reserved liquid to make 1 cup. (If you don't have enough liquid from the oranges add some water.) Add oranges and nuts to mixture. Bake in greased muffin tins at 350 degrees for 25-30 minutes. For glaze combine sugar, oil and vanilla. Add water to make right consistency for a glaze. Spread on cooled muffins.

Yield: 36 muffins

Family Secret: We like these best after they have been frozen. They seem to have a better flavor and are more moist.

Happiness may be thought, sought or caught, but not bought.

BLUEBERRY MUFFINS

1 cup margarine
3 cups sugar
2 teaspoons vanilla
8 eggs
5 cups flour

2 tablespoons baking soda
$^1/_2$ teaspoon salt
$2^1/_4$ cups sour cream
$3^1/_2$ cups fresh or frozen
   blueberries

Cream together margarine and sugar. Add vanilla and eggs. Mix well. Sift together flour, baking soda and salt. Stir this into egg mixture alternately with sour cream. Fold in blueberries. Fill greased muffin tins about $^3/_4$ full. Bake at 375 degrees for 30-40 minutes.

Yield: 60 muffins

PUMPKIN APPLE STREUSEL MUFFINS

$2^1/_2$ cups flour
2 cups sugar
1 tablespoon pumpkin pie
   spice
1 teaspoon baking soda
$^1/_2$ teaspoon salt

2 eggs
$^3/_4$ cup cooked pumpkin
$^1/_2$ cup vegetable oil
2 cups peeled, chopped
   apples

STREUSEL TOPPING:
2 tablespoons flour
$^1/_4$ cup sugar

$^1/_2$ teaspoon cinnamon
2 teaspoons butter, softened

In a large bowl combine flour, sugar, spice, baking soda and salt. In another bowl beat eggs, pumpkin and oil. Add to dry ingredients and stir until moistened. Stir in apples. Fill greased muffin tins about $^3/_4$ full. Combine topping ingredients and sprinkle on top. Bake at 350 degrees for 35-40 minutes.

Yield: 36 muffins

Jesus is the bridge over troubled waters.

RHUBARB MUFFINS

1 1/4 cups brown sugar
1/2 cup vegetable oil
1 egg
2 teaspoons vanilla
1 cup buttermilk
1 1/2 cups diced rhubarb

1/2 cup chopped walnuts
2 1/2 cups flour
1 1/2 teaspoons baking soda
1/2 teaspoon baking powder
1/2 teaspoon salt

TOPPING:
1 teaspoon melted
   margarine

1/3 cup sugar
1 teaspoon cinnamon

In a large bowl combine sugar, oil, egg, vanilla and buttermilk. Stir in rhubarb and nuts. In a smaller bowl combine flour, soda, baking powder and salt. Add to rhubarb mixture. Spoon batter into greased muffin tins. Mix topping ingredients and sprinkle on top of batter. Bake at 375 degrees for 20-25 minutes.

Yield: 2 1/2 dozen muffins

ZUCCHINI MUFFINS

3 eggs
1 3/4 cups sugar
1 cup vegetable oil
3 teaspoons vanilla
2 cups flour
1 tablespoon cinnamon

1 teaspoon baking soda
1 teaspoon salt
2 cups peeled, grated
   zucchini
1 cup chopped nuts

In a large mixing bowl beat together eggs, sugar, vegetable oil and vanilla. In separate bowl mix flour, cinnamon, baking soda and salt. Stir into egg mixture. Add zucchini and nuts. Fill greased muffin pans 2/3 full and bake at 350 degrees for 25-30 minutes.

Yield: 3 dozen

Family Secret: Do you have an overabundance of zucchini like Lois usually does? Then try these muffins! They are very good and moist.

Happiness can be multiplied by dividing.

BUTTERMILK BISCUITS

4 cups flour
1 1/2 teaspoons salt
2 teaspoons baking powder

1 teaspoon baking soda
1/4 cup shortening
2 cups buttermilk

Combine dry ingredients. Add shortening and blend with pastry blender. Add buttermilk and stir until dough follows spoon around bowl. Turn out on a well floured surface and knead for 1/2 minute. Roll 1/2 inch thick, fold, cut and bake on ungreased pan at 450 degrees for 12-15 minutes.

Yield: 12-14 biscuits

EASY DROP BISCUITS

4 cups Bisquick
3 eggs

1/2 teaspoon salt
1 cup milk

Combine Bisquick, eggs and salt. Add milk and mix well. Drop on an ungreased cookie sheet and bake at 400 degrees for 10-12 minutes.

Yield: 3-4 dozen

Ivan & Sara Ann Miller
Charm, Ohio

BACON, EGG AND CHEESE CASSEROLE

$^1/_2$ pound bacon
8 slices white bread
$^1/_2$ pound Velveeta cheese
6 eggs

2 cups milk
$^1/_2$ teaspoon salt
$^1/_4$ teaspoon dry mustard

Cut bacon in small pieces and fry until crisp. Cut bread slices in cubes and place in a greased 2 quart casserole dish. Cube or shred cheese and put on top of bread. In blender or mixing bowl beat eggs, milk, salt and mustard. Pour over bread and cheese. Sprinkle bacon pieces on top. Cover and refrigerate overnight. Bake, covered, at 350 degrees for 50-60 minutes or until puffed up. Serve immediately.

Yield: 8 servings

Family Secret: This casserole comes in handy when you have overnight guests. Try sausage or ham instead of bacon for a different flavor.

BARBEQUED HAM SLICES

$^1/_4$ cup chopped onions
2 tablespoons butter
$^1/_2$ cup catsup
$^1/_3$ cup water
2 tablespoons brown sugar

2 tablespoons white vinegar
1 tablespoon Worcestershire
   sauce
12 thick slices boneless ham

Sauté onions in butter and add the rest of the ingredients and bring to a boil. Simmer for 5 minutes. Arrange slices of ham in a small roaster. Pour sauce over ham, cover and bake at 350 degrees for 2 hours.

Yield: 12 whole slices or 24 halves

Family Secret: This is very good and tender and takes little time to prepare. Great for Sunday dinner! Can be prepared the day before, then just pop into oven before leaving for church!

BREAKFAST BURRITOS

16 ounces frozen hash
   browns
1 pound cooked ham, cut in
   small cubes
1 small onion, chopped
1 green pepper, diced

8 eggs
12 flour tortillas
2 cups shredded Velveeta
   cheese
Salsa
Sour cream

In a large skillet fry hash browns, ham, onion and green pepper. Beat eggs and pour in separate skillet. Cook and stir until set. Remove from heat. Add to hash brown mixture and mix gently. Place about $3/4$ cup of filling on each tortilla and top with some shredded cheese. Roll up and place in a greased baking pan. Bake at 350 degrees for 15-20 minutes. Serve with salsa and sour cream.

Yield: 12 servings

HASH BROWNS

4 cups cooked, shredded
   potatoes
2 tablespoons butter
1 tablespoon vegetable oil

$1/2$ teaspoon paprika
$1/2$ teaspoon salt
$1/2$ teaspoon seasoned salt

Melt butter in skillet with vegetable oil. Sprinkle $1/4$ teaspoon paprika in skillet. Arrange potatoes evenly in skillet; sprinkle with remaining paprika, salt and seasoned salt. Brown lightly. Remove from skillet and place in a glass baking dish. Bake in 350 degree oven for 20 minutes.

Yield: 4-6 servings

Family Secret: If you have leftover hash browns or just want something different add some chopped onions before baking and put cheese slices on top during the last 5 minutes in oven.

Kindness is the oil that takes the friction out of life.

BARBEQUED SAUSAGE

2 pounds sausage links or
   patties
2 tablespoons butter
1/2 cup catsup

2 tablespoons prepared
   mustard
2 tablespoons brown sugar
1 teaspoon Worcestershire
   sauce

Brown sausage in butter. Combine rest of ingredients. Arrange sausage in a baking dish. Brush sauce liberally on each piece. Cover and bake at 350 degrees for 1 hour.

Yield: 8-10 servings

SAUSAGE GRAVY

2 pounds bulk sausage
1/4 cup butter or margarine
1 1/4 cups flour
2 quarts milk

Salt
Seasoned salt
Black pepper

Cook sausage in butter until browned on medium heat. Add flour and stir in well. Gradually add 1 1/2 quarts of the milk. Continue to heat and keep stirred. It will thicken as it cooks. Add more milk if necessary to make it right consistency. Continue to cook awhile after right consistency is reached. Add seasonings according to your taste. Serve with biscuits or hash browns.

Yield: 12-15 servings

Family Secret: The cook never has to worry about sampling the gravy when Paul's around! It seems he always knows when the gravy is ready! Actually, it's a favorite with all the men in the family.

No one knows what he can do until he tries.

FAMILY CHEESE SAUCE

2 cups sour cream
1 pound Velveeta cheese

2 tablespoons butter
Milk

Combine sour cream, cubed cheese and butter in saucepan. Heat on low, stirring often, until cheese is melted. Add small amount of milk for right consistency.

Yield: 4 cups

Family Secret: Our guests like this sauce on scrambled eggs, hash browns and our bacon, egg and cheese casserole. We also like it on vegetables and mashed potatoes.

NUTTY BAKED FRENCH TOAST

1 loaf white bread, sliced
8 eggs
2 cups milk
2 cups half and half

2 teaspoons vanilla
$^1/_2$ teaspoon nutmeg
$^1/_2$ teaspoon cinnamon

NUT TOPPING:
$^3/_4$ cup butter, softened
$1^1/_3$ cups brown sugar
3 tablespoons dark corn
    syrup

$1^1/_3$ cups coarsely chopped
    nuts

Generously grease two 11x8x2 inch baking pans. Fill pans with bread slices to within $^1/_2$ inch of top. Blend together eggs, milk, half and half, vanilla, nutmeg and cinnamon. Pour over bread slices. Cover and refrigerate overnight. Combine topping ingredients and set aside until time to bake toast. Spread topping over toast. Bake at 350 degrees for 50 minutes until puffed and golden. If top browns too quickly cover with foil.

Yield: 10-12 servings

Family Secret: It has become a tradition for our family to spend the night of Christmas Eve at the Inn and we love waking up to this on Christmas morning!

CRUNCHY CRUST FRENCH TOAST

1 egg
$^1/_3$ cup milk
2 teaspoons sugar
$^1/_4$ teaspoon cinnamon
$^1/_3$ cup crushed corn flakes

3 tablespoons butter or
    margarine
4 slices white bread
    (homemade works great)

Blend egg, milk, sugar and cinnamon. Dip bread slices in egg mixture then coat with corn flake crumbs. Melt butter in skillet over medium heat. Brown prepared slices in skillet until light golden on both sides. Sprinkle with powdered sugar and serve with maple syrup.

Yield: 4 servings

FLUFFY PANCAKES

2 cups Bisquick
2 eggs

$^1/_2$ cup milk
$^1/_2$ cup lemon lime soda

Combine all ingredients and mix well. Pour on greased, hot griddle and fry. Very light and fluffy pancakes.

Yield: 12-15 pancakes

Family Secret: The lemon lime soda makes these pancakes very light and fluffy.

RAISED FLAPJACKS

1 package dry yeast
$^1/_4$ cup warm water
1 egg

$1^1/_3$ cups milk
2 cups Bisquick

In mixing bowl dissolve yeast in warm water. Add egg, milk and Bisquick. Beat until smooth. Cover and let stand for $1^1/_2$ hours or refrigerate 8 hours. Pour on greased, hot griddle and fry.

Yield: 12-15 flapjacks

FRUIT PIZZA

CRUST:
2 cups Bisquick
1/3 cup sugar
1 egg

1/3 cup melted butter or
   margarine

FILLING:
8 ounces cream cheese,
   softened
1/2 cup sugar
1 teaspoon vanilla
8 ounces whipped topping

Fresh or canned fruits
   (peach slices, pineapple,
   oranges, grapes, apples,
   blueberries, kiwi, etc.)

PINEAPPLE GLAZE:
1 1/4 cups pineapple juice
1/4 cup orange juice
1/3 cup sugar

1/4 cup clear jel
3/4 cup water

Mix crust ingredients to form a soft dough. Pat dough in a greased 12 inch round pizza pan. Bake at 375 degrees until edges begin to brown, 10-12 minutes. Cool completely. Cream together cream cheese, sugar and vanilla until smooth. Beat in whipped topping. Spread over cooled crust to within 1/4 inch of rim. Then arrange fruits decoratively on top of filling. In a medium saucepan combine pineapple juice, orange juice and sugar. Bring to a boil. Combine clear jel and water and stir until smooth. Gradually add this to pineapple juice, stirring constantly. Cook until clear. Cool. Spread over fruit.

Yield: 8-12 servings

Family Secret: Fruit pizza is a favorite with our guests as well as our family. Marvin, especially, is very well known for cleaning up any leftover fruit pizza! We get more requests for it than anything else we serve for breakfast! The bulk food stores in our area have clear jel—the thickening this recipe calls for. We like it because it turns clear when you cook it.

Daily prayers diminish your daily cares.

BUTTERY CINNAMON SKILLET APPLES

$^1/_3$ cup butter	$^1/_2$ teaspoon cinnamon
$^1/_2$ cup white sugar	$1^1/_2$ cups water
2 tablespoons brown sugar	4 medium cooking apples,
2 tablespoons cornstarch	peeled and sliced

In 10 inch skillet melt butter over medium heat. Stir in sugars, cornstarch and cinnamon. Blend in water. Arrange apples over sauce. Cover and cook over medium heat, spooning sauce over apples occasionally until apples are fork tender and sauce is thickened (12-20 minutes).

Yield: 6-8 cups

Family Secret: These are delicious served on pancakes! It sure doesn't take much syrup when you put these on your pancakes. Our family likes to add a scoop of vanilla ice cream on top yet!

FRUIT SLUSH

2 cups sugar	6-8 bananas, sliced
3 cups boiling water	20 ounces crushed
12 ounces frozen orange juice	pineapple
concentrate	18 ounces lemon lime soda

Dissolve sugar in boiling water. Add orange juice concentrate, bananas and pineapple, stirring until orange juice is dissolved. Stir in soda. Pour into a large container or several small containers and freeze. Thaw in refrigerator approximately 1 hour, or until slushy before serving. For variation add fresh sliced peaches or seedless grapes.

Yield: 10-12 servings

Family Secret: Assembled and frozen ahead, this refreshing mix can feature fruits in season. Tastes so good on a hot summer day. Try freezing in individual cups for a quick snack or freeze in a large bowl for an evening cookout.

In His will is our peace.

TROPICAL FRUIT DESSERT

1¹/₄ cups sugar
¹/₂ cup clear jel
1 envelope tropical punch
　　drink mix
4 cups water

1 can pineapple tidbits,
　　drained
6 bananas
1 cup red seedless grapes

In a medium saucepan combine sugar, clear jel and drink mix. Stir in water. Boil over medium heat, stirring constantly, until clear. Remove from heat and cool. Chill in refrigerator then add pineapple, sliced bananas and grapes.

Yield: 8-10 servings

Family Secret: A quick and easy dessert that adds color to any meal. We especially like this on pancakes!

PUMPKIN CINNAMON ROLLS

²/₃ cup milk
4 tablespoons butter
1 cup pumpkin
4 tablespoons sugar
1 teaspoon salt
2 eggs

2 packages yeast
4 cups flour
2 tablespoons melted butter
¹/₂ cup brown sugar
2 teaspoons cinnamon

In a small saucepan heat milk and 4 tablespoons butter until warm (110-115 degrees). In a bowl combine pumpkin, sugar and salt. Add the milk mixture. Beat in eggs and yeast. Add flour. Mix, then cover and let rise until double. Turn out onto a floured surface and knead until smooth. Roll out into a rectangular shape. Brush on the melted butter. Mix cinnamon and sugar and sprinkle on. Roll dough jelly roll style, starting with the long end. Slice into 1 inch circles. Place individually on lightly greased cookie sheets or in round pans with slices almost touching. Let rise in a warm place until double. Bake at 350 degrees for 20 minutes. Frost, if desired.

Yield: 2 dozen

MOM'S CINNAMON ROLLS

1 package yeast
1 cup warm milk
$^1/_4$ cup white sugar
$2^1/_2$ cups flour, divided
1 teaspoon salt

2 beaten eggs
$^1/_4$ cup melted butter
$^1/_4$ cup brown sugar
1 teaspoon cinnamon

Dissolve yeast in milk. Add white sugar and 1 cup flour. When bubbly add salt, eggs, butter and remaining flour. Just stir until well mixed. Place in a lightly greased bowl with lid and let rise in a warm place until double in size. Punch down and roll out on floured surface. Mix brown sugar and cinnamon and sprinkle on dough. Roll up as you would for a jelly roll. Cut in slices and place in baking pan, sides almost touching. Let rise until about double in size again. Bake at 425 degrees for 8-10 minutes. Ice with your favorite icing.

Yield: 12-15 rolls

LOIS' CINNAMON ROLLS

1 cup scalded milk
$^1/_2$ cup sugar
$1^1/_2$ teaspoons salt
$^1/_4$ cup shortening
$^1/_4$ cup vegetable oil
5 teaspoons yeast

1 cup warm water (110-115 degrees)
2 beaten eggs
7 cups flour
$^1/_2$ teaspoon nutmeg

Pour scalded milk over sugar, salt, shortening and vegetable oil. Let cool to lukewarm. Meanwhile dissolve yeast in warm water. Add beaten eggs; beat well. Add yeast and egg mixture to cooled milk mixture. Add half of the flour and nutmeg and stir. Add remaining flour and knead until well mixed. Place in a greased bowl. Cover and let rise until double, about 2 hours. Divide in 4 equal parts and roll out on a greased surface to $^1/_4$ inch thick. Spread lightly with melted butter and sprinkle with a little white sugar and cinnamon. Roll lengthwise as you would a jelly roll; cut with a sharp knife about $^1/_4$-$^1/_2$ inch thick slices. Place in greased pans and let rise until double, about 1 hour. Bake at 350 degrees for 15 minutes or until done. Ice with your favorite icing.

Yield: 3-4 dozen

PLUCKETS

16 ounces frozen bread dough,
   partially thawed
$^1/_2$ cup chopped walnuts
3 ounces butterscotch pudding
   (not instant)

1 cup brown sugar
$^1/_2$ cup butter
1 teaspoon cinnamon
1 teaspoon vanilla
$^1/_2$ cup milk

Grease a large bread pan. Sprinkle nuts on bottom. In a medium saucepan combine pudding, sugar, butter, cinnamon, vanilla and milk. Bring to a boil and boil for 3-5 minutes. Let cool then pour 1 cup of pudding mixture over nuts. Cut bread dough into cubes and place on top. Pour remaining pudding mixture over dough. Cover with wax paper and refrigerate overnight. Bake, uncovered, at 350 degrees for 30 minutes. Remove from oven and invert onto serving plate almost immediately.

Yield: 6-8 servings

Family Secret: Add a good flavor to your morning coffee break with these tasty rolls.

PEACHES 'N CREAM COFFEE CAKE

$^2/_3$ cup flour
1 teaspoon baking powder
$^1/_2$ teaspoon salt
1 egg
$^1/_2$ cup milk
CREAM FILLING:
8 ounces cream cheese,
   softened
$^1/_2$ cup sugar
TOPPING:
1 tablespoon sugar

3 tablespoons melted butter
1 large can sliced peaches or
   $2^1/_2$ cups sweetened
   fresh peaches

3 tablespoons reserved
   peach juice

$^1/_2$ teaspoon cinnamon

Mix flour, baking powder and salt. Add egg, milk and butter and beat for 2 minutes. Pour into a well greased 8 inch round pan. Drain peaches, reserving juice. Arrange peaches on top of batter. Cream together filling ingredients. Spoon cream cheese mixture on top of fruit to within $^1/_2$ inch of edge. Combine sugar and cinnamon. Sprinkle on top. Bake at 350 degrees for 30-35 minutes.

Yield: 8 servings

WALNUT WONDER COFFEE CAKE

2 cups flour
1 teaspoon baking powder
1 teaspoon baking soda
$1/2$ teaspoon salt
1 cup margarine

1 cup sugar
2 eggs
1 teaspoon vanilla
1 cup sour cream

CRUMB NUT TOPPING:

$1/3$ cup brown sugar
$1/4$ cup white sugar
1 teaspoon cinnamon

1 cup chopped nuts
$1/3$ cup chocolate chips

Combine flour, baking powder, soda and salt. Cream together margarine and sugar and stir eggs and vanilla into creamed mixture. Add sour cream alternately with dry ingredients. Spread batter in a greased 13x9x2 inch pan or two 8 inch round pans. In separate bowl mix ingredients for topping and sprinkle mixture over batter. Bake at 350 degrees for 35 minutes.

Yield: 16-20 servings

Family Secret: Ivan will do almost anything for one of these cakes with the following creamy filling! This is the kind of cake he requests for his birthday!

CREAMY COFFEE CAKE FILLING

$1/2$ cup shortening
1 cup marshmallow creme
2 cups powdered sugar

1 teaspoon vanilla
Milk

Cream shortening and marshmallow creme. Add powdered sugar and vanilla and enough milk to make right consistency for spreading. This is good in almost any coffee cakes, especially in the Walnut Wonder. Just slice cakes in half, spread filling on bottom half and put top layer back on.

Yield: enough for 2 coffee cakes

FINNISH COFFEE CAKE

CAKE:

1¼ cups sugar
1 cup vegetable oil
2 eggs
1 teaspoon vanilla
1 cup buttermilk
2¼ cups flour

½ teaspoon salt
½ teaspoon baking powder
½ teaspoon baking soda
4 tablespoons brown sugar
1 tablespoon cinnamon

GLAZE:

2 cups powdered sugar
4 teaspoons vanilla

Hot water to make right
consistency for drizzling
over cake

Beat together sugar, oil, eggs, vanilla and buttermilk. Then add flour, salt, baking powder and soda. Mix well. Pour half of batter into a greased 13x9x2 inch pan. Combine brown sugar and cinnamon; sprinkle half on batter. Pour rest of batter on top and sprinkle with rest of sugar and cinnamon. Bake at 350 degrees for 30-35 minutes. When done, poke holes in cake with a fork and drizzle with glaze while still hot.

Yield: 24 pieces

Don't wait for a crisis to discover what is important in your life.

HOMEMADE GRANOLA CEREAL

8 cups quick oats
1 teaspoon salt
1 cup brown sugar
1 1/2 teaspoons baking soda
1 cup maple syrup

1 cup whole wheat flour
1 cup melted butter
22 graham crackers, crushed
1/2 cup chopped nuts
1/2 cup chocolate chips

Combine oats, salt, sugar, soda, maple syrup, flour and butter. Put on cookie sheets and toast in oven until nicely browned, approximately 1 hour at 250 degrees. Add crackers and nuts for the last 15 minutes of baking time. When still warm, but not hot, add chocolate chips.

Yield: approximately 15 cups

Family Secret: This is delicious with milk but we also like it as a topping on fruit or ice cream.

BAKED OATMEAL

1/2 cup melted butter
3/4 cup brown sugar
2 beaten eggs
1 teaspoon salt

3 cups quick oats
1 teaspoon cinnamon
2 teaspoons baking powder
1 cup milk

Mix everything together and pour in a greased 8 inch square pan. Bake at 350 degrees for 30 minutes. Serve warm with milk.

Yield: 6-8 servings

Family Secret: This hits the spot on cold winter mornings.

Everyone lives in one of two tents, either content or discontent.

Pictured on Reverse Side

Mom's Homemade Bread
Banana Nut Bread
Cornmeal Dinner Rolls

Entrance, bridge and winding driveway.

FRESH
BAKED
BREADS

FRESH BAKED BREADS

BANANA BREAD

8 ounces cream cheese,
   softened
1 cup sugar
$^1/_4$ cup margarine, room
   temperature
1 cup mashed bananas

2 eggs
$2^1/_4$ cups flour
$1^1/_2$ teaspoons baking powder
$^1/_2$ teaspoon baking soda
1 cup chopped nuts

Combine cream cheese, sugar and margarine. Mix until well blended. Blend in bananas and eggs. Add dry ingredients, mixing until moistened. Fold in nuts. Pour into greased and floured 9x5x3 inch loaf pan. Bake at 350 degrees for 1 hour.

Yield: 1 loaf

CHEDDAR CORN BREAD

$^3/_4$ cup cornmeal
$^1/_2$ cup flour
4 tablespoons sugar
1 teaspoon salt
$^1/_2$ teaspoon baking powder
1 teaspoon baking soda
2 eggs, beaten

$1^1/_4$ cups buttermilk
$^1/_4$ cup vegetable oil
$^1/_2$ cup shredded Cheddar
   cheese
$8^3/_4$ ounces cream style
   corn

In a mixing bowl combine first six ingredients. In a separate bowl combine remaining ingredients. Add to dry ingredients and stir only until moistened. Pour into a greased nine inch square baking pan. Bake at 350 degrees for 30-35 minutes or until bread is golden brown and tests done.

Yield: 8-10 servings

If at first you don't succeed—you're running about average.

CORN BREAD

1/2 cup shortening
1/2 cup brown sugar
2 eggs
1 1/4 cups cornmeal
1 1/2 cups flour

1 teaspoon salt
1 teaspoon baking powder
1 teaspoon baking soda
1 cup buttermilk

Cream sugar and shortening. Add eggs and beat until smooth. Combine dry ingredients and add alternately with buttermilk. Put in a greased 11x7x2 inch pan. Bake at 350 degrees for 20 minutes. Cut in squares. Serve warm with lots of butter!

Yield: 10-12 servings

CORNMEAL DINNER ROLLS

1/3 cup cornmeal
1/2 cup sugar
2 teaspoons salt
1/2 cup melted margarine
2 cups milk

2 beaten eggs
1 package yeast
1/4 cup warm water
4 cups flour

In saucepan combine cornmeal, sugar, salt, margarine and milk. Cook until thick. Cool to lukewarm. Dissolve yeast in warm water. Add yeast mixture and eggs to cooked mixture. Let rise 2 hours. Knead in flour and let rise another hour. Roll out on floured surface and cut with biscuit cutter. Place rolls on baking sheet and let rise 1 hour. Bake at 375 degrees for 15 minutes.

Yield: 30 rolls

The nice thing about being imperfect is the joy it brings to others.

FROZEN CRESCENT ROLLS

2 cups milk
2 packages yeast
1 cup sugar
1 cup shortening
2 teaspoons salt

6 beaten eggs
9 cups flour, divided
$^1/_2$ cup melted butter or
    margarine

Heat milk to 110-115 degrees. Add yeast; stir until dissolved. In large mixing bowl cream sugar, shortening and salt. Add eggs; mix well. Add half the flour, then add milk mixture, mixing until flour is moistened. Add remaining flour by hand. On floured surface knead until smooth and elastic, 6-8 minutes. Place dough in greased bowl; cover and let rise until double, about $1^1/_2$ hours. Divide dough into 4 parts. Roll each into a circle and brush with melted butter. Cut each circle into 16 pie shaped pieces. Roll each piece into a crescent, starting at wide end. Place on baking sheet and freeze immediately. When frozen place in plastic bags. Store in freezer until ready to use. To bake, place on a greased baking sheet and cover. Let rise until double, about 3-4 hours. Bake at 350 degrees for 12-15 minutes.

Yield: 64 crescent rolls

MELT-IN-YOUR-MOUTH DINNER ROLLS

1 package yeast
$^1/_2$ cup warm water
1 tablespoon sugar
1 teaspoon baking powder
1 cup milk

$^1/_3$ cup margarine
$^1/_3$ cup sugar
Pinch of salt
2 beaten eggs
$4^1/_2$ cups flour

Dissolve yeast in warm water. Add sugar and baking powder. Let set for 20 minutes. Scald milk. Add margarine, sugar and salt. Cool then add eggs. Add to yeast mixture. Mix in flour. Cover and refrigerate overnight. Roll out 2 hours before serving and shape either as butterhorns or pinwheels in muffin pans. Let rise until double. Bake at 400 degrees for 10-15 minutes. Brush with melted butter.

Yield: 2 dozen

OATMEAL DINNER ROLLS

1 cup quick oats
2 cups boiling water
3 tablespoons butter
$^2/_3$ cup brown sugar
1 tablespoon white sugar

$1^1/_2$ teaspoons salt
2 packages yeast
$^1/_3$ cup warm water
5 cups flour

In saucepan combine first three ingredients and cook until thickened. Let cool until lukewarm. Dissolve yeast in warm water. Add sugars and salt then stir yeast mixture into oat mixture. Knead in flour. Let rise in a covered bowl until double. Form into dinner rolls and place on baking sheet. Let rise again until double then bake at 350 degrees for 20-30 minutes.

Yield: 2-2$^1/_2$ dozen

BUTTERHORNS

$1^1/_2$ packages yeast
1 tablespoon sugar
1 cup warm milk (110-115
    degrees)
$^1/_2$ cup margarine, room
    temperature

4 cups flour
2 teaspoons salt
$^1/_4$ cup sugar
3 eggs, slightly beaten

Dissolve yeast and sugar in warm milk. Combine margarine, flour, salt and sugar. Work together as for pie dough. Add beaten eggs to milk mixture. Pour into flour mixture and stir until it holds together. Refrigerate overnight. In morning cut dough in half. Roll out into a circle. Cut into 8 pie shaped wedges. Roll each wedge into butterhorn shape. Let rise until light to touch. Bake at 375 degrees for 12-15 minutes. Brush with melted butter.

Yield: 16 rolls

---

*Wouldn't it be nice if we could sell our mistakes for
what they cost us.*

ZUCCHINI BREAD

3 eggs
1³/₄ cups sugar
1 cup vegetable oil
3 teaspoons vanilla
2 cups flour
1 tablespoon cinnamon

1 teaspoon baking soda
1 teaspoon salt
2 cups peeled, grated
   zucchini
1 cup chopped nuts

In a large mixing bowl beat together eggs, sugar, vegetable oil and vanilla. In separate bowl mix flour, cinnamon, baking soda and salt. Stir into egg mixture. Add zucchini and nuts. Pour into greased 9x5x3 inch loaf pan and bake at 350 degrees for 25-30 minutes.

Yield: 1 loaf

Leon & Lois Mast
'The Inn Farmhouse'

LOIS' HOMEMADE BREAD

11 1/2 teaspoons yeast
1/2 teaspoon brown sugar
3/4 cup warm water
1/2 cup melted margarine
1 cup milk, scalded

1 cup white sugar
1/2 cup vegetable oil
8 teaspoons salt
4 1/4 cups hot tap water
18 cups flour

Dissolve yeast and brown sugar in 3/4 cup warm water. Combine the rest of the ingredients in a large mixing bowl with 10 cups flour on top. Make a well into flour with spatula and pour yeast mixture in. Stir thoroughly. Knead in remaining flour until right texture. Knead for another 10 minutes. Cover and let rise until double. Punch down then let rise until double again. Form into 9 or 10 loaves and put in greased pans. Let rise until double. Bake at 350 degrees for 25-30 minutes. For whole wheat bread subtract 4 cups of the white flour and use 4 cups whole wheat flour instead.

Yield: 9 or 10 loaves

MOM'S HOMEMADE BREAD

3 packages yeast
3 cups warm water
1/3 cup brown sugar
1/3 cup white sugar

1 1/2 tablespoons salt
3 tablespoons flour
3/4 cup vegetable oil
8 cups flour

Dissolve yeast in water. Mix sugars, salt and 3 tablespoons flour. Add to yeast mixture. Stir, then add oil and gradually work in flour. Place in a lightly greased bowl; cover and let rise 1/2 hour. Punch down then let rise another 1/2 hour. Work dough again then let rise for 1 hour. Punch down and form into 5 or 6 loaves. Put in greased pans and let rise approximately 1 hour or until raised 1/2 inch above pan. Bake at 325 degrees for 30 minutes.

Yield: 5 or 6 loaves

PEANUT BUTTER SPREAD

1/2 cup peanut butter
1 1/4 cups white corn syrup

1 cup marshmallow creme

Mix well. Delicious on any bread but especially on homemade!

Yield: 2 3/4 cups

Pictured on Reverse Side

*A spring photo of walkway leading
to front porch and entrance.*

*Dorothy's Domain, one of fifteen guest rooms,
all with private baths, air-conditioning, quilts, etc.*

SOUPS
AND
SALADS

SOUPS

SALADS

BROCCOLI SOUP

1 small can chicken broth
10 ounces chopped broccoli
    fresh or frozen, use more
    or less according to taste
2 chicken bouillon cubes
3 tablespoons butter or
    margarine

$^1/_4$ cup chopped onions
4 tablespoons flour
$^1/_8$ teaspoon pepper
$^1/_2$ teaspoon salt
$2^1/_4$ cups milk
1 cup Velveeta cheese

In a large saucepan bring chicken broth, broccoli and chicken flavored bouillon cubes to a boil, then simmer till broccoli is tender. In another large pan melt butter or margarine. Sauté onions in butter then add flour, pepper and salt. Stir until thick, then add milk and Velveeta cheese. Now add milk mixture to broccoli and leave on low heat till cheese is melted. Optional: You can add 1 cup leftover mashed potatoes (the more you add the thicker the soup), or cook noodles with the broccoli. This also makes it thicker.

Yield: 6-8 servings

CHEESE SOUP

4 chicken bouillon cubes
1 quart water
1 cup chopped celery
1 small onion, chopped
1 cup diced carrots
1 cup diced potatoes

10 ounces frozen mixed
    vegetables
2 cans cream of chicken
    soup
2 cans water
1 pound Velveeta cheese

Boil bouillon, water, celery and onion for 20 minutes. Add potatoes, carrots and mixed vegetables. Cook until tender. Add soup, water and cheese. Heat on low until cheese melts.

Yield: 6-8 servings

CHEESY POTATO BACON SOUP

6 large potatoes, diced
$^1/_8$ cup chopped onion
1 teaspoon salt
2 quarts milk
Dash pepper

$^1/_2$ pound Velveeta cheese,
   more or less as desired
1 pound bacon, fried and
   crumbled

Cook potatoes and onion in salt water until tender. Drain and lightly mash potatoes. Add milk and pepper. Bring to a boil. (If not thick enough make white sauce with cornstarch and thicken to right consistency.) Add cheese and bacon. Heat until cheese is melted. Serve with crackers or toasted bread cubes.

Yield: 6-8 servings

CHICKEN RICE SOUP

2 46 ounce cans chicken
   broth
1 teaspoon salt
$^1/_4$ teaspoon pepper
2 teaspoons instant chicken
   bouillon
1$^1/_2$ cups chopped carrots
2 cups rice

2 tablespoons butter
3 cups chopped celery
1 cup chopped onion
2 10 ounce cans cream of
   mushroom soup,
   undiluted
4 cups cooked, cut up
   chicken

In large kettle place chicken broth, salt, pepper, bouillon, carrots and rice. Bring to a boil and simmer until carrots and rice are tender. Melt butter in skillet; add celery and onion and sauté 3 minutes. Add to broth and rice mixture. Stir in mushroom soup and chicken and heat through, being careful not to scorch. If soup is too thick, add more broth.

Yield: 12-15 servings

One who is faithful in a very little thing is faithful in much.

CHILI SOUP

1 pound ground beef
1 small onion, chopped
2 tablespoons butter
$1/2$ cup flour
$1/2$ cup brown sugar
2 cups water

1 15 ounce can kidney
   beans
Chili seasoning, salt and
   pepper to taste
1 quart tomato juice

Brown beef and onion in butter in medium kettle. Add flour and sugar and brown just a little. Slowly stir in water. Add beans, seasonings and tomato juice. Simmer for 15 minutes.

Yield: 6-8 servings

Family Secret: We like our chili served over cooked rice and topped with corn chips and sour cream.

HAMBURGER SOUP

1 pound ground beef
1 cup chopped onions
$1/2$ cup green peppers,
   optional
2 cups tomato juice
1 cup diced carrots

1 teaspoon salt
$1/8$ teaspoon pepper
1 teaspoon seasoned salt
1 cup diced potatoes
$1/3$ cup flour
1 quart milk

In large kettle, brown beef with onions and peppers. Stir in tomato juice, carrots and seasonings. Cover and cook until carrots are partly done. Add potatoes and cook until vegetables are tender. Combine flour with 1 cup milk and stir into soup. Add rest of milk. Heat to boiling; simmer for 2-3 minutes.

Yield: 6 servings

Before giving someone a piece of your mind make sure you can spare it!

HAM 'N BEAN SOUP

1 pound dried Great Northern
    beans
1 meaty ham bone
3 quarts water
1 chopped onion

3 cups chopped celery
2 cups mashed potatoes
Salt and pepper
$1/4$ pound Velveeta cheese

Place beans and enough water to cover in a large saucepan. Bring to a boil and boil for 2 minutes. Remove from heat and soak for 1 hour. Drain and rinse beans. In a large kettle place beans and ham bone in 3 quarts water. Bring to a boil. Reduce heat; cover and simmer for 2 hours. Add onion, celery, potatoes, salt and pepper. Simmer 1 hour longer. Remove ham bone from the soup. Remove meat from the bone; dice and return to kettle. Add cheese and heat on low until cheese is melted.

Yield: 8-10 servings

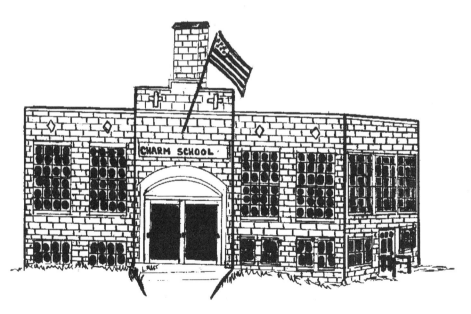

CHARM SCHOOL
This is where all of us children went to school (Charm, Ohio)

BROCCOLI SALAD

1 head cauliflower
2 bunches broccoli
1 pound bacon, fried and
    crumbled

8 ounces shredded Cheddar
    cheese
$^1/_2$ cup slivered almonds,
    toasted in butter

DRESSING:
1 cup salad dressing
$^3/_4$ cup vegetable oil
$^1/_4$ cup water
1 cup sugar

$^1/_4$ cup vinegar
2 teaspoons prepared
    mustard

Wash cauliflower and broccoli. Cut in bite size pieces. Drain and add bacon, cheese and almonds. Blend together dressing ingredients. Pour over vegetables and toss.

Yield: 10 servings

BLUEBERRY JELLO SALAD

2 3 ounce packages grape
    jello
2 cups boiling water

1 20 ounce can crushed
    pineapple
1 can blueberry pie filling

TOPPING:
8 ounces cream cheese
1 cup powdered sugar

1 cup sour cream
8 ounces whipped topping

Mix jello and water and stir until jello is dissolved. Add pineapple and pie filling. Pour into a pan or mold. Chill until set. Mix together cream cheese and powdered sugar. Fold in sour cream and whipped topping. Spread on top of set jello.

Yield: 10-12 servings

Draw near to God and He will draw near to you.
James 4:8

COTTAGE CHEESE SALAD

1 3 ounce box lemon or lime
   jello
1 1/2 cups boiling water
1 cup cottage cheese

1 cup drained crushed
   pineapple
1/2 cup sugar
2 cups whipped topping

Dissolve jello in water. Let stand until it starts to thicken. Combine cottage cheese, pineapple and sugar; stir into jello. Fold in whipped topping. Pour in a glass bowl or pan and chill until firm.

Yield: 4-6 servings

CREAMY COLESLAW

1 small head cabbage,
   shredded
1/3 cup sugar

1 teaspoon salt
1 tablespoon vinegar

DRESSING:
1 cup salad dressing
1/3 cup sugar

1/2 teaspoon prepared
   mustard
1/2 cup whipped topping

Mix cabbage, sugar, salt and vinegar and let stand for 30 minutes. Combine dressing ingredients, folding whipped topping in last. Pour over cabbage and mix gently. Chill and serve.

Yield: 6-8 servings

Family Secret: Naomi likes to add some fried, crumbled bacon and fresh chopped red or green pepper to this recipe just before serving. Try it!

*You can't push yourself ahead by patting yourself
on the back.*

COLESLAW

1 medium head cabbage,
   shredded
1 carrot, shredded
1 green pepper, chopped
1 teaspoon salt

1 cup vinegar
$^1/_4$ cup water
2 cups sugar
1 teaspoon celery seed
1 teaspoon mustard seed

Combine cabbage, carrot, pepper and salt. Let stand for 1 hour. In saucepan combine rest of ingredients and boil together for 1 minute. Cool, then pour over cabbage and stir. Put in glass jars or freezer boxes and freeze.

Yield: 10-12 servings

DELUXE MACARONI SALAD

$^1/_2$ pound small shell
   macaroni
5 hard-boiled eggs
3 tablespoons chopped
   onion
1 cup chopped celery

1 cup cooked, diced chicken
1 cup semi-cooked frozen or
   canned peas, drained
1 cup cubed or shredded
   cheese

DRESSING:
$^3/_4$ cup salad dressing
1 tablespoon prepared
   mustard
$^1/_2$ teaspoon salt

2 tablespoons milk
$1^1/_2$ teaspoons vinegar
$^3/_4$ cup sugar

Cook, drain and rinse macaroni. Add diced eggs, onion, celery, chicken, peas and cheese. Combine dressing ingredients and fold into macaroni mixture. Refrigerate overnight.

Yield: 8-10 servings

Family Secret: A simple and delicious salad to make for potlucks and summer picnics!

LAYERED LETTUCE SALAD

1 medium head lettuce
1 small head cauliflower
1 1/2 cups frozen peas
4 hard-boiled eggs, diced
1 pound bacon, fried and
    broken in pieces

2 cups salad dressing
1 tablespoon brown sugar
4 ounces shredded Cheddar
    cheese

Chop lettuce in bite size pieces and place in a rectangular pan. Cut up cauliflower and layer on lettuce. Then layer frozen peas, eggs and bacon on cauliflower. Combine salad dressing and sugar. Spread on salad ingredients like you would frost a cake. Top with shredded cheese. Refrigerate for 6-8 hours before serving.

Yield: 10-12 servings

LIME SALAD

CRUST:
2 cups flour
1/2 cup brown sugar

1/2 cup chopped walnuts
1 cup butter, softened

FILLING:
1 3 ounce package lime jello
1 20 ounce can crushed
    pineapple, drain,
    reserving juice

8 ounces cream cheese,
    softened
1 cup sugar
1 12 ounce can evaporated
    milk, chilled

Combine crust ingredients and press into a 13x9x2 inch pan. Bake at 350 degrees for 12-15 minutes. In saucepan bring reserved pineapple juice to a boil. Remove from heat and stir in jello; dissolve then cool. Cream together cream cheese and sugar. Blend in jello. Stir in pineapple. Whip evaporated milk and fold into mixture. Pour on top of cooled crust. Chill and serve.

Yield: 16-20 servings

A true friend can hear a tear drop.

POTATO SALAD

12 cups potatoes, cooked and shredded
8 hard-boiled eggs, chopped

$^1/_2$ small onion, chopped
$1^1/_2$ cups chopped celery

Combine:

3 cups salad dressing
6 tablespoons mustard
$^1/_4$ cup vinegar

$2^1/_4$ cups sugar
4 teaspoons salt
$^1/_2$ cup milk

Pour dressing over potato mixture. Mix gently. Refrigerate. This actually is better if prepared a day or two ahead of time.

Yield: 3$^1/_2$ quarts

RAINBOW JELLO MOLD

1 3 ounce package cherry jello
1 3 ounce package orange jello
1 3 ounce package lime jello
$4^1/_2$ cups boiling water, divided
$^1/_4$ cup sugar

1 cup pineapple juice
1 3 ounce package lemon jello
$^1/_2$ cup cold water
3 ounces cream cheese
2 cups whipped topping

Prepare each package (cherry, orange and lime) jello with $1^1/_2$ cups boiling water. Pour in shallow pans and chill until set. Heat pineapple juice to boiling then add sugar and lemon jello. When jello is dissolved add cold water. Blend in the cream cheese and whipped topping. Cut set jello into small cubes and fold into the mixture. Pour into mold and refrigerate until set.

Yield: enough for one 5 cup mold

Forget your mistakes but remember what they taught you.

TACO SALAD

1 pound ground beef
1 small onion, diced
1 package taco seasoning
   mix
1 medium head lettuce,
   chopped
2 large tomatoes, chopped

2 cups shredded Cheddar
   cheese
1 12-16 ounce bag taco
   flavored chips, crushed
16 ounces French dressing
1/4 cup taco sauce

Brown hamburger and onion in skillet. Add taco seasoning mix. Set aside to cool. Toss chopped lettuce with tomatoes and cheese. Add beef mixture and taco chips. Combine French dressing and taco sauce. Add to lettuce mixture and toss gently. The ingredients of this salad may be prepared ahead of time but do not combine them longer than 15-30 minutes before you are ready to serve.

Yield: 8-10 servings

VEGETABLE PIZZA

2 packages refrigerated
   crescent rolls
8 ounces cream cheese,
   softened
1 cup mayonnaise
1 package dry buttermilk
   dressing mix

1 cup each of finely chopped
   broccoli, cauliflower and
   tomatoes
1/2 cup each of finely chopped
   peppers, carrots and
   onions
4 ounces shredded Cheddar
   cheese
1/4 cup bacon bits, optional

Unroll crescent rolls and spread in a single layer in a greased 15x10 inch jelly roll pan. Press seams to seal. Bake at 375 degrees for 8-10 minutes. Beat together cream cheese, mayonnaise and dressing mix. Spread on cooled crust. Arrange vegetables, more or less as desired, on top of cream cheese mixture. Press in gently. Sprinkle cheese and bacon bits on top. Chill. Cut in squares and serve.

Yield: 24 squares

Wit without wisdom is like salt without meat.

THREE BEAN SALAD

1 can yellow wax beans
1 can green beans
1 can kidney beans
¹/₂ cup sliced or chopped
    onions

¹/₄ cup chopped green or red
    peppers
¹/₂ cup vinegar
¹/₂ cup sugar
¹/₂ cup vegetable oil

Drain all the beans. Combine with onions and peppers. Mix vinegar, sugar and oil. Pour over beans and mix well. Chill overnight before serving. This salad remains tasty a long time if it is refrigerated.

Yield: 6-8 servings

THREE LAYER JELLO SALAD

LAYER #1:
1 6 ounce box lime jello
1 20 ounce can crushed
    pineapple, drain,
    reserving juice

¹/₂ cup chopped pecans

Prepare jello according to package directions, adding pineapple and pecans when slightly thickened. Pour into an 8x8 inch pan and chill until set.

LAYER #2:
8 ounces cream cheese,
    softened

¹/₂ cup sugar
2 cups whipped topping

Beat together cream cheese and sugar. Add whipped topping and mix. Spread on top of set jello.

LAYER #3:
Reserved pineapple juice,
    plus water to make 1
    cup

1 cup sugar
1 tablespoon flour
1 egg, beaten

Mix together in a saucepan and cook over medium heat until thickened. Remove from heat and cool. Spread chilled sauce over layer #2. Refrigerate.

Yield: 8-10 servings

SWEET 'N SOUR SALAD DRESSING

1 cup salad dressing
3/4 cup vegetable oil
1/4 cup water
1 cup sugar

1/4 cup vinegar
2 teaspoons prepared
    mustard, optional

Mix together until well blended. Our favorite dressing for lettuce salads.

Yield: 3 1/4 cups

Family Secret: Carol especially likes this dressing. When she makes it she always makes several batches right away! She likes lots of it on her salads and also on rice!

THOUSAND ISLAND DRESSING

1 cup salad dressing
1/2 cup sugar
1/4 cup catsup

1/4 cup pickle relish
1/4 teaspoon salt
Dash pepper

Combine and stir until well blended. Serve on lettuce salad.

Yield: 2 cups

So faith, hope, love abide, these three: but the greatest of these is love. I Corinthians 13:13

Pictured on Reverse Side

Mom's Homemade Bread
Pan Fried Chicken
Dressing
Mashed Potatoes
Chicken Gravy
Mixed Vegetables with Cracker Crumbs
Potato Salad
Mom's Meat Loaf
Sweet & Sour Salad Dressing
Lettuce Salad

A view from the front porch of the Inn.

FAVORITE
MAIN
DISHES

FAVORITE MAIN DISHES

BEEF

PORK

CHICKEN

VEGETABLES

BAKED BEANS

32 ounce can pork 'n
   beans
16 ounce can kidney
   beans
16 ounce can butter beans
1 small onion, chopped

1 pound bacon, fried and
   broken in pieces
$^1/_4$ cup bacon drippings
1 cup catsup
1 cup brown sugar
1 tablespoon prepared
   mustard

Mix all together and stir gently. Bake in a casserole dish at 350 degrees for 50-60 minutes.

Yield: 8 servings

Family Secret: We love to top these beans with crushed corn chips and sour cream! And for something different and tasty add one 15$^1/_2$ ounce can pineapple tidbits before baking. Delicious!

BARBEQUED GREEN BEANS

10 slices bacon
$^1/_4$ cup chopped onion
$^3/_4$ cup catsup
$^1/_2$ cup brown sugar

3 teaspoons Worcestershire
   sauce
$^3/_4$ teaspoon salt
4 cups green beans

Fry bacon then break in pieces. In 2 tablespoons bacon fat, sauté chopped onions. Combine catsup, brown sugar, Worcestershire sauce and salt. Add onions and bacon pieces. Pour over green beans and mix lightly. Bake in a 1 quart covered casserole dish at 300 degrees for 35-40 minutes or until heated through.

Yield: 4-6 servings

A truly rich child is one whose parents love one another.

BROCCOLI CASSEROLE

1 cup water
1/2 teaspoon salt
1 cup rice
1/4 cup butter
1/4 cup chopped onion
1/4 cup chopped celery
1 can cream of mushroom
    soup

1 can cream of celery soup
10 ounce package frozen
    chopped broccoli, thawed
1/2 cup Velveeta cheese
1 can French fried onions

Bring water and salt to a boil. Add rice; cover and remove from heat. Let set for 5 minutes. Melt butter in skillet. Sauté onion and celery until tender. In large bowl combine rice, celery and onion with the soups, broccoli and cheese. Pour into a greased casserole. Top with French fried onions. Bake at 350 degrees for 1 hour.

Yield: 6 servings

CABBAGE SUPREME

1 medium head cabbage
1/4 cup chopped green pepper
1/4 cup chopped onion
1 tablespoon butter
1/2 teaspoon salt
1/8 teaspoon pepper

2 cups milk
1/2 cup shredded Cheddar
    cheese
1/4 cup butter
1/4 cup flour
1/4 cup mayonnaise

Cut cabbage into 8 wedges. In a large, covered skillet cook cabbage in a small amount of water about 12 minutes. Drain. Place in a 13x9x2 inch baking pan. In saucepan cook peppers and onion in butter until tender. Blend in flour, salt and pepper. Add milk and 1/4 cup butter; cook and stir until bubbly. Pour over cabbage. Bake uncovered in 375 degree oven for 20 minutes. Combine cheese and mayonnaise and spoon on wedges. Bake 5 more minutes.

Yield: 8 servings

MIXED VEGETABLE CASSEROLE

2$^1/_2$ pounds frozen mixed
   vegetables
1 tablespoon salt
$^1/_4$ cup butter

$^1/_2$ pound Velveeta cheese
2 cups crushed Ritz crackers
3 tablespoons melted butter

Cook vegetables in salt water until tender. Drain. In saucepan melt $^1/_4$ cup butter. Add cheese and melt over low heat. When melted, gently stir into the vegetables and place in a baking pan. Combine crushed crackers and 3 tablespoons melted butter and sprinkle on top of vegetables. Bake, uncovered, at 350 degrees for 10-15 minutes.

Yield: 8-10 servings

DELICIOUS MASHED POTATOES

3 pounds potatoes
8 ounces cream cheese,
   softened
$^1/_4$ cup butter

$^1/_2$ cup sour cream
2 eggs
$^1/_2$ cup milk
1 teaspoon salt

Peel and cook potatoes until tender. In a large bowl mash the hot potatoes. Cut cream cheese into small pieces and add to potatoes along with butter. Beat well then add sour cream. Beat eggs, milk and salt together then add to potatoes. Beat well. Pour mixture in a greased 2 quart casserole. Cover and refrigerate overnight. Bake at 350 degrees for 45 minutes.

Yield: 8 servings

The greatest power we can find in the world is God's love.

PARMESAN POTATOES

$^1/_3$ cup butter
$^1/_4$ cup flour
$^1/_4$ cup Parmesan cheese
Salt and seasoned salt to taste

6 medium potatoes, washed
and peeled
Sour cream

Melt butter on cookie sheet in oven. Combine flour, cheese and salt. Cut potatoes in wedges and soak in water then dip in flour mixture. Bake on cookie sheet at 375 degrees for 1 hour or until golden, turning once. Serve with sour cream.

Yield: 8 servings

STUFFED BAKED POTATOES

4 large baking potatoes
4 tablespoons butter
$^1/_2$ cup cream
2 tablespoons chopped
onion

$^1/_2$ cup shredded Cheddar
cheese
$^1/_2$ teaspoon salt
Paprika

Bake potatoes until done. While warm cut a slice off the top of each potato and scoop out pulp leaving a $^1/_4$ inch thick shell. Using mixer beat the pulp, butter and cream. Beat until smooth. Stir in onion, cheese and salt. Place the shells on a baking sheet and fill with pulp mixture. Sprinkle with paprika and bake at 375 degrees for 25-30 minutes.

Yield: 4 servings

Family Secret: When Mom has a special dinner planned and has lots of last minute preparations, she likes to prepare these the day before and they're ready to just pop into the oven!

The only thing achieved in life without effort is failure.

HARVARD BEETS

3 cups cooked beets
$^1/_2$ cup sugar
1 tablespoon cornstarch
1 teaspoon salt

$^1/_4$ cup vinegar
$^1/_4$ cup water
2 tablespoons butter

Combine sugar, cornstarch and salt. Add the vinegar and water and stir until smooth. Pour in a medium saucepan. On medium heat bring to a boil and cook for 5 minutes, stirring often. Add beets to hot sauce, cover and let stand for 30 minutes. Before serving bring to a boil and add butter.

Yield: 6 servings

CONEY SAUCE

2 tablespoons margarine
2 tablespoons flour
1 pound ground beef
1 cup catsup
$^1/_2$ cup barbeque sauce

1 tablespoon prepared
  mustard
1 teaspoon brown sugar
2 tablespoons diced onion
2 tablespoons chopped
  green pepper

In a medium saucepan lightly brown margarine. Stir in flour. Brown ground beef in margarine mixture then add the rest of the ingredients. Heat and simmer for about an hour. Serve on hot dogs.

Yield: 10-12 servings

STEAK MARINADE

1 cup soy sauce
$^1/_2$ cup vegetable oil
1 teaspoon ginger
1 teaspoon dry mustard

1 teaspoon seasoned salt
  flavor enhancer
$^1/_4$ teaspoon garlic salt
3-6 whole cloves

Mix well and marinate your steaks for 12-24 hours before grilling.

Yield: enough for 4-6 steaks

SAUCY MEATBALLS

MEATBALLS:

1 pound ground beef
$^1/_2$ cup dry bread crumbs
$^1/_4$ cup milk
1 egg, beaten
$^1/_4$ teaspoon salt

$^1/_2$ teaspoon Worcestershire
   sauce
2 tablespoons chopped
   onion

SAUCE:

1 can cream of mushroom
   soup
$^1/_3$ cup milk

$^1/_8$ teaspoon ground nutmeg
$^1/_2$ cup sour cream

Mix ingredients for meatballs. Shape into 20 $1^1/_2$ inch balls. Bake in an ungreased 13x9x2 inch pan for 20 minutes at 400 degrees. In a casserole dish mix soup, milk and nutmeg. Add meatballs to sauce. Bake at 350 degrees for 30 minutes. Remove and top with sour cream. Serve.

Yield: 20 meatballs

Ole Mill Furniture
Charm, Ohio

HAMBURGER CASSEROLE

2 pounds ground beef
1 cup chopped onions
1 can cream of chicken soup
2 cans cream of mushroom soup
1 pint peas

8 ounces fine noodles,
   cooked
Buttered bread crumbs
Velveeta cheese slices

Brown beef and onions in a large skillet. Stir in soups, peas and cooked noodles. Pour in a greased 3 quart casserole dish. Top with bread crumbs. Cover and bake 30 minutes at 350 degrees then place cheese slices on top and bake another 20 minutes.

Yield: 6-8 servings

RICE AND HAMBURGER CASSEROLE

$^3/_4$ cup uncooked converted
   rice
1 pound ground beef,
   browned
1 cup chopped onion

$^1/_4$ teaspoon black pepper
1 can cream of chicken soup
1 can cream of mushroom
   soup
$2^1/_2$ soup cans water

Mix all together. Pour in a greased casserole dish and bake, uncovered, at 350 degrees for 1 hour. If too thick add a little more water. If desired serve with chow mein noodles on top.

Yield: 6-8 servings

Let prayer be the key of the morning and the bolt of the evening.

TATER AND HAMBURGER CASSEROLE

2 pounds ground beef
Salt and pepper
1 quart cooked green beans,
    drained

1 can cream of mushroom
    soup
1/2 pound Velveeta cheese
1 pound package frozen
    Tater Tots

Mix raw beef with salt and pepper. Press into a 13x9x2 inch pan. Place green beans on beef then soup and a thick layer of cheese. Arrange Tater Tots on top. Cover and bake at 350 degrees for 1 hour or until done.

Yield: 8-10 servings

BURRITO CASSEROLE

1 pound ground beef
15 ounce can refried beans
1 envelope taco seasoning
    mix
8 small flour tortillas
1 pint sour cream

1 can cream of mushroom
    soup
Shredded Cheddar cheese
Chopped tomatoes
Chopped lettuce
Salsa
Additional sour cream

Fry ground beef. Add beans and taco seasoning. Spread 1 heaping tablespoon on each tortilla and roll up. Mix sour cream and cream of mushroom soup. Spread some on bottom of a baking pan. Lay burritos on top. Spread remaining soup mixture on top of burritos. Bake at 350 degrees for 30 minutes; add shredded cheese on top and return to oven long enough for cheese to melt. Serve with tomatoes, lettuce, salsa and sour cream.

Yield: 8 servings

There is no failure except in no longer trying.

HAYSTACK

3 cups crushed Ritz crackers
4 cups cooked rice
1 medium head lettuce, chopped
3 chopped tomatoes
1½ cups diced green pepper
1½ cups diced onion
2 cups shredded carrots
12 ounce package shredded Cheddar cheese

1 pound ground beef, browned and mixed with 1 quart spaghetti sauce
2 cans Cheddar cheese soup, mixed with 1 can milk, 1 cup sour cream and 1 pound Velveeta cheese
3 cups crushed taco flavored chips

Prepare ingredients as stated. (The rice, spaghetti sauce and cheese soup are served hot.) Serve in the order given and place a little of everything on top of each other on your plate. Your "haystack" may get pretty large! Dig in and enjoy!

Yield: 8-10 servings

Family Secret: You can add or subtract from this list of ingredients. The amounts given here are based on what our family likes. You may have to adjust! If you don't care for cheese sauce a sweet and sour salad dressing is good on it, too. This is a fun meal to make for a large group.

HUSBAND'S DELIGHT

8 ounces cream cheese
2 cups sour cream or 1 cup
   milk
1 small onion, chopped
1 1/2 pounds ground beef
2 tablespoons butter
16 ounces tomato sauce
1 teaspoon sugar

1 teaspoon salt
Dash pepper
1/2 teaspoon Worcestershire
   sauce
10 ounces noodles
1/2 cup shredded Velveeta
   cheese

In a large bowl mix softened cream cheese, sour cream and onion. Brown meat in butter. Add tomato sauce, sugar, salt, pepper and Worcestershire sauce. Cook noodles according to package directions. In a greased 2 quart casserole dish layer cooked noodles, beef mixture and sour cream mixture. Top with shredded cheese and bake at 350 degrees until lightly browned on top.

Yield: 6-8 servings

MOCK TURKEY

1 loaf bread
2 pounds ground beef
1 small onion
2 cans cream of chicken soup

1 can cream of celery soup
2 cups milk
Salt to taste

Cut bread in cubes, place on a baking sheet and toast in a 350 degree oven. Fry ground beef with onion. Drain off grease. Mix toasted bread cubes, ground beef, soups, milk and salt together. Pour in a greased casserole dish and bake, covered, at 325 degrees for 1 hour.

Yield: 6-8 servings

A sharp tongue and a dull mind are often found in the same head.

MOM'S MEAT LOAF

3 pounds ground beef
1¹/₂ - 2 cups tomato juice
4 eggs
4 teaspoons salt
¹/₂ teaspoon pepper

Seasoned salt, to taste
1¹/₂ cups finely crushed
   crackers
¹/₄ cup chopped onions

BARBEQUE SAUCE:
1 cup catsup
¹/₃ cup brown sugar

2 teaspoons prepared
   mustard

Beat together tomato juice, eggs and seasonings. Mix into raw ground beef. Add crushed crackers and onions. In a greased loaf pan shape into a loaf and bake uncovered at 350 degrees for 1 hour. Mix sauce ingredients and brush on top during last 15 minutes of baking.

Yield: 8-10 servings

PIZZA CASSEROLE

1 pound ground beef
1 small onion, chopped
1 tablespoon butter
10 ounces shell macaroni
2 cans pizza sauce
4 ounces sliced pepperoni

1 small can mushroom
   pieces
4 ounces shredded
   mozzarella cheese
Velveeta cheese slices

Brown beef and onion in butter. Add salt and pepper to taste. Cook macaroni according to package directions. Mix everything together except cheese. Pour in a greased casserole dish and top with cheese. Bake at 350 degrees for 45 minutes.

Yield: 6 servings

Wealth is not what we have, but what we are.

PIZZA CRUST

1 cup warm water
1 tablespoon yeast (or 1
    package)
2 tablespoons sugar

2 tablespoons vegetable oil
2¹/₂ cups flour
1 teaspoon salt

Dissolve yeast in warm water. Add the other ingredients and let stand 5 minutes. Press in a lightly greased pizza pan. Add your favorite pizza toppings and bake at 375 degrees for 25-30 minutes.

Yield: 1 crust

PIZZA LOAF

1¹/₂ pounds ground beef
8 ounces tomato sauce
¹/₄ cup chopped onions
1 beaten egg
³/₄ cup quick oats
1 tablespoon Worcestershire
    sauce

1¹/₂ teaspoons salt
¹/₂ teaspoon oregano
¹/₄ teaspoon pepper
6 ounces shredded
    mozzarella cheese

Combine all ingredients except cheese. Pat half of mixture into a lightly greased oblong pan. Put cheese (reserve a few tablespoons) on top then cover with other half of beef mixture. Bake uncovered at 350 degrees for 1 hour. Sprinkle reserved cheese on top a few minutes before serving.

Yield: 6 servings

Of all the things you wear your expression is most important.

POTATO/CARROT CASSEROLE

1 1/2 pounds ground beef
1/4 cup chopped onion
1 tablespoon butter or
    margarine
Salt and pepper
5 cups sliced or cubed
    potatoes

2 cups sliced carrots
1 can cream of mushroom
    soup
1 can water
1/4 pound Velveeta cheese

Brown ground beef and onion in butter. Add salt and pepper. In a greased casserole, layer potatoes, carrots and ground beef. Combine soup and water and pour over top. Cover with cheese slices. Cover and bake at 350 degrees for 1 hour or until potatoes and carrots are tender.

Yield: 8 servings

TATER TOT CASSEROLE

2 pounds ground beef
1 cup cracker crumbs
1/4 cup chopped onion
Salt and pepper

1 can cream of mushroom
    soup
1 can Cheddar cheese soup
2 pound package frozen
    Tater Tots

Mix ground beef, cracker crumbs, onion, salt and pepper. Press into a 13x9x2 inch pan. Mix the soups together. Spread on beef mixture. Arrange Tater Tots on top. Cover and bake at 350 degrees for 50 minutes. Uncover and bake another 15-20 minutes.

Yield: 10 servings

STUFFED GREEN PEPPERS

6 large green peppers
1 1/2 pounds ground beef
1 cup cornflake crumbs
1/2 cup cooked rice
2 beaten eggs

1 teaspoon salt
1 teaspoon seasoned salt
11 ounce can tomato soup
1/2 cup water

Cut tops off peppers and remove seeds. Cook peppers in salt water for 5 minutes then drain. Combine raw beef, cornflake crumbs, rice, eggs, salt and seasoned salt. Stuff peppers with meat mixture and place in a baking dish. Mix tomato soup and water and pour over peppers. Bake, uncovered, at 350 degrees for 45 minutes.

Yield: 6 servings

STUFFED SHELL CASSEROLE

1 box large shell macaroni
1 1/2 cups cooked rice
2 pounds ground beef
2 eggs
1 cup oatmeal

1 teaspoon salt
1/4 teaspoon pepper
1 1/2 quarts spaghetti sauce
4 ounces shredded
    mozzarella cheese

Cook macaroni in salt water until tender then drain and cool. Beat eggs and combine with oatmeal, rice, salt and pepper. Mix this into raw ground beef. Stuff shells with beef mixture. Place in a lightly greased 13x9x2 inch pan. Pour spaghetti sauce over the stuffed shells and sprinkle cheese on top. Bake at 350 degrees for 45 minutes.

Yield: 12-16 servings

It's difficult to keep your mind and your mouth open at the same time.

TACO PIE

1 can refrigerated crescent
   rolls
1 pound ground beef
1 package taco seasoning
   mix
1/2 cup catsup

6 slices Velveeta cheese
Chopped lettuce
1 chopped tomato
French dressing
Sour cream

Heat oven to 400 degrees. Press crescent rolls into a pie pan. Bake 8-10 minutes or until golden. Brown meat and add taco seasoning and catsup. Put on top of baked crust. Place cheese slices on top and return to oven just until cheese is melted. Cut in wedges and put chopped lettuce and tomatoes on top. Serve with French dressing and sour cream.

Yield: 6 servings

YUM-E-ZETTI

1 1/2 pounds ground beef
2 tablespoons margarine
12 ounces wide noodles
1 cup chopped celery

1 can cream of mushroom
   soup
8 ounces pizza sauce
1/2 pound Velveeta cheese
Salt, according to taste

Brown meat in margarine. Cook noodles until tender but not soft. Combine meat, noodles, celery, undiluted soup, pizza sauce and salt. Place in a 1 1/2 quart casserole dish and top with sliced cheese. Cover and bake at 350 degrees for 45-50 minutes.

Yield: 8 servings

LOIS' YUMEZETTI

16 ounces noodles, medium
    or wide
2 pounds ground beef
1 medium onion, chopped
$^1/_2$ cup chopped celery

Salt and pepper to taste
2 cans cream of mushroom
    soup
$1^1/_2$-2 cans evaporated milk

Cook noodles until tender but not real soft. Drain and rinse slightly. Cook ground beef with onion, celery and a little water. Add salt and pepper. Drain beef and combine with noodles. Add soup and milk. Put half of mixture in greased casserole dish, then a layer of cheese, then rest of noodle mixture and remaining cheese on top. Cover and bake at 325 degrees for 1-$1^1/_2$ hours.

Yield: 8-10 servings

SLOPPY JOES

6 pounds ground beef
3 cups quick oats
4 cups catsup
2 cups water

12 tablespoons chopped
    onion
8 tablespoons brown sugar
12 tablespoons vinegar

In a large kettle cook beef until almost done; add oats. Mix rest of ingredients and pour over meat mixture; stir. Bake 1 hour at 350 degrees. Serve on buns.

Yield: 50-60 sandwiches

Treasure is not always a friend, but a friend is always a treasure.

SWISS SUPPER LOAF

1 large loaf homemade bread
   or 16 ounce loaf Italian
   bread
$^1/_2$ cup salad dressing
2 tablespoons prepared
   mustard

$^1/_2$ pound each of 3 different
   kinds of thinly sliced
   luncheon meat
Sliced Swiss cheese
Sliced tomatoes and
   onions, optional
Lettuce leaves, optional

Preheat oven to 400 degrees. Being careful not to cut quite all the way through, cut bread into $^1/_2$ inch slices. Combine salad dressing and mustard; spread on both sides of bread slices. Tuck meat and a slice of Swiss cheese between bread slices. Wrap loaf with foil. Bake 15-20 minutes until cheese is melted and loaf is heated through. To serve, remove foil; complete cutting through loaf to separate into slices. Serve with tomatoes, onions and lettuce if desired.

Yield: 4-6 servings

SCALLOPED POTATOES WITH HAM

$2^1/_2$ pounds potatoes
$^1/_2$ cup butter
2 cans cream of chicken
   soup
$^1/_2$ pound Velveeta cheese

$1^1/_2$ cups sour cream
Salt and pepper
$1^1/_2$ pounds cooked ham
2 tablespoons melted butter
2 cups cornflake crumbs

Wash, peel and cook potatoes. Cool, then shred or slice. Melt $^1/_2$ cup butter in a medium saucepan. Add soup, cheese, sour cream, salt and pepper. Heat until cheese is melted, stirring constantly. Pour over potatoes. Cut ham in $^1/_2$ inch cubes and stir into potatoes. Mix well then place in a large greased casserole. Combine melted butter and cornflake crumbs. Put on top and bake, covered, for 45 minutes at 350 degrees. Uncover and bake another 10 minutes or until heated through.

Yield: 10-12 servings

HAM LOAF

LOAF MIXTURE:

5 pounds ham loaf mix
3 eggs
1 tablespoon baking powder

$1^1/_4$ cups milk
$1^2/_3$ cups cornflake crumbs

PINEAPPLE GLAZE:

$2^2/_3$ cups brown sugar
4 teaspoons dry mustard

2 cups pineapple juice

Mix the loaf ingredients well. Pat into a well greased roaster or casserole dish. Divide down the center forming 2 loaves. Combine glaze ingredients and pour over meat. Bake at 350 degrees for $1^1/_2$-2 hours. Baste every 30 minutes with glaze.

Yield: 15 servings

NOODLE FRANKFURTER BAKE

8 ounce package noodles
$^1/_4$ cup margarine
2 tablespoons flour
1 cup milk
1 cup Velveeta cheese
$^1/_2$ teaspoon salt

1 pound frankfurters, sliced
$^1/_4$ cup brown sugar
1 tablespoon prepared
   mustard
$^1/_4$ cup salad dressing
1 package frozen Tater
   Tots, optional

In a large kettle cook noodles according to package directions. Drain, and return to kettle. In a saucepan melt margarine. Stir in flour. Add milk, cheese and salt. Heat until cheese is melted. Stir sauce and frankfurters into noodles. Combine brown sugar, mustard and salad dressing. Stir into noodles. Pour into a 13x9x2 inch pan. Arrange Tater Tots on top and bake uncovered at 375 degrees for 30-35 minutes. When not using Tater Tots, spread salad dressing mixture on top of noodles and bake.

Yield: 10 servings

OVEN BARBEQUED CHICKEN

1 fryer chicken (3 pounds)
  or equivalent pieces
1 1/2 cups flour

4 tablespoons margarine
Salt, pepper and seasoned
  salt

BARBEQUE SAUCE:
1 medium onion, chopped
2 tablespoons vegetable oil
2 tablespoons vinegar
2 tablespoons brown sugar
1/4 cup lemon juice
1 cup catsup

3 tablespoons
  Worcestershire sauce
1/2 tablespoon prepared
  mustard
1 cup water

Dip chicken pieces in flour and brown in melted margarine. Arrange pieces in a baking pan and season with salt, pepper and seasoned salt according to taste. Sauté onion in oil then add the rest of sauce ingredients. Simmer sauce for 30 minutes. Pour over chicken. Bake, uncovered, at 325 degrees for 1 hour.

Yield: 4 servings

BAKED CHICKEN CASSEROLE

9 slices bread
4 cups cooked chicken
2 tablespoons butter
1 cup chopped celery
4 eggs
2 cups milk (or part chicken
    broth)

2 cans cream of mushroom
    soup
1/2 cup mayonnaise
Velveeta cheese

Grease a 6 quart roaster or casserole dish. Cut bread in 1 inch cubes and place evenly in roaster. Layer cut up chicken on bread. Sauté celery in butter and place on chicken. Beat eggs, milk, mushroom soup and mayonnaise. Pour over casserole. Cover with cheese slices. Bake, covered, at 350 degrees for 1 1/2-2 hours on until puffed up and firm.

Yield: 10-12 servings

CHICKEN RICE CASSEROLE

2 cups rice
2½ cups chicken broth
1 cup chopped celery
2 tablespoons chopped onion
2 tablespoons butter or margarine

2 cups cream of mushroom soup, undiluted
1½ cups mayonnaise
2 cups cooked chicken, diced
1 cup cornflake crumbs
2 tablespoons butter or margarine, melted

Cook rice in chicken broth on low heat for 20 minutes, covered. Sauté celery and onion in butter. Combine mushroom soup, mayonnaise and chicken. Add this and the sautéed mixture to cooked rice. Mix gently. Place in a greased casserole dish. Mix cornflake crumbs and melted butter and pat on top. Cover and bake at 350 degrees for 45 minutes.

Yield: 6-8 servings

COUNTRY CHICKEN AND BISCUITS

2½ cups diced, cooked chicken
1½ cups Velveeta cheese, cubed
1-2 cans cream of chicken soup

10 ounces frozen mixed vegetables
2 cups cubed potatoes
Salt and seasoned salt
1 can oven ready biscuits

In a 2½-3 quart casserole dish combine chicken, cheese and soup. Cook mixed vegetables and potatoes until tender. Add salt and seasoned salt. Add vegetables to chicken; mix and bake, covered, for 20 minutes at 350 degrees. Arrange biscuits on top; leave uncovered and return to oven; bake 20 minutes longer at 375 degrees or until biscuits are done.

Yield: 4-6 servings

Man sees your actions, but God sees your motives.

DRESSING

1 loaf bread
1 cup chopped carrots
2 cups chopped celery
2 cups diced potatoes
2 cups chicken pieces

6 eggs
2 cups milk (or part broth)
2 tablespoons chicken
    flavored base
Salt and pepper to taste

Cut bread in 1/2 inch cubes and put in a jelly roll pan or cake pan. Place in 350 degree oven, stirring occasionally, until lightly toasted. Cook the carrots, celery and potatoes, separately, until tender. Drain. In a large mixing bowl combine toasted bread cubes, vegetables and chicken. Beat together eggs, milk and seasonings. Pour over other mixture. Let stand for at least 1/2 hour. Taste to see if more seasoning is needed. Melt some butter or margarine in a large skillet. Pour dressing into skillet and on medium heat brown lightly. Place in a covered casserole dish and bake at 350 degrees for 45-60 minutes. Garnish with parsley.

Yield: 10-12 servings

CHICKEN TETRAZZINI

1/4 cup butter
1/4 cup flour
1/2 teaspoon salt
1/4 teaspoon pepper
1 cup chicken broth
1 cup half and half cream

1 can cream of mushroom
    soup
1/2 cup Velveeta cheese
1/2 pound spaghetti, cooked
    and drained
2 cups cooked chicken

Melt butter in a large saucepan over low heat. Blend in flour, salt and pepper. Cook over low heat, stirring until smooth and bubbly and slightly browned. Remove from heat. Stir in broth, cream, soup and cheese; heat to boiling. Boil and stir for 1 minute. Stir in spaghetti and chicken. Pour into a lightly greased 2 quart casserole dish. Bake, uncovered, for 30 minutes at 350 degrees.

Yield: 6-8 servings

CHICKEN CRESCENTS

2 cups diced, cooked
chicken
3 ounces cream cheese
3/4 cup cream of chicken soup
2 teaspoons milk
1/4 teaspoon salt

1/8 teaspoon pepper
8 ounce can refrigerated
crescent rolls
2 tablespoons melted butter
2 cups crushed seasoned
croutons

In a medium bowl mix chicken, cream cheese, soup, milk, salt and pepper. Separate crescent rolls so that you have 4 rectangles; press each very flat. Spoon 1/2 cup chicken mixture onto half of each rectangle. Fold other half over and seal edges. Brush top and bottom with melted butter and roll each crescent in crushed croutons. Place on a cookie sheet and bake at 350 degrees for 25 minutes.

Yield: 4 servings

CHICKEN GRAVY

4 1/2 cups chicken broth (may
be part water)
1 1/2 tablespoons chicken
flavored seasoning
1/8 teaspoon garlic salt

5 tablespoons clear jel
2 tablespoons flour
1 egg yolk
1/2 cup milk

In a medium saucepan combine broth, seasoning and garlic salt. Bring to a boil; remove from heat. Mix clear jel and flour; add a little milk and stir. Add egg yolk and rest of milk. Gradually stir into hot broth. Return to low heat and continue stirring until thickened.

Yield: 5 cups

Quarrels wouldn't last long if the fault was only on one side.

Pictured on Reverse Side

Chocolate Peanut Butter Pie
Graham Cracker Pudding
Angel Food Cake with Butter Cream Frosting
Cherry Pie with Nut Topping
Date Pudding
Cream Cheese Pecan Pie

A fall scene overlooking buildings of the Inn's farm.

DELICIOUS
DESSERTS

DELICIOUS DESSERTS

APPLE CRISP

1 cup sugar, divided
2 teaspoons lemon juice
$^1/_4$ cup water
$^1/_2$ teaspoon cinnamon
6 tart apples, peeled

$^3/_4$ cup flour
$^1/_4$ teaspoon salt
6 teaspoons butter, room
  temperature

Combine $^1/_2$ cup sugar, lemon juice, water and cinnamon in an 11x7x2 inch baking pan. Slice apples into pan and mix. Blend remaining $^1/_2$ cup sugar, flour, salt and butter until crumbs form. Spread over apples; pat smooth. Bake at 375 degrees about 40-45 minutes until apples are tender and crust nicely brown. Serve warm with ice cream or whipped topping.

Yield: 8 servings

BROWNIE ICE CREAM ROLL

$1^1/_2$ cups sugar
1 cup Bisquick
$^3/_4$ cup chopped nuts
$^3/_4$ cup melted butter
$1^1/_2$ teaspoons vanilla

3 eggs
3 ounces melted
  unsweetened chocolate
1 quart vanilla ice cream
Powdered sugar

Heat oven to 350 degrees. Line 15x10 inch jelly roll pan with aluminum foil. Grease foil. Mix all ingredients except last two. Beat vigorously. Spread in pan; bake until set, about 25 minutes. Cool brownie in pan on wire rack. Invert on rack or cookie sheet. Remove foil. Cut brownie crosswise in three equal parts. Place one part of brownie on plate. Spread with half of ice cream. Top with another brownie, then the remaining ice cream and brownie on top. Sprinkle with powdered sugar. Wrap and freeze until firm, 8 hours. Remove from freezer and cut into slices. Top with hot fudge and serve.

Yield: 8-10 slices

Tact is the talent to have less to retract.

CAROL'S ICE CREAM DESSERT

1 cup chocolate chips
$^1/_2$ cup margarine
1$^1/_2$ cups powdered sugar
1$^1/_2$ cups evaporated milk
1 teaspoon vanilla

15 graham crackers, crushed
$^1/_2$ cup melted margarine
$^1/_2$ cup sugar
$^1/_2$ gallon vanilla ice cream,
    softened

In saucepan combine chocolate chips, margarine, powdered sugar and milk. Cook until thick, stirring constantly. Cool, then add vanilla. Combine crushed crackers, margarine and sugar. Press in bottom of 13x9x2 inch pan, reserving 1 cup crumbs for the top. Cover with ice cream. Freeze until firm. Pour chocolate mixture over top and sprinkle with reserved crumbs. Return to freezer.

Yield: 15-20 servings

CHOCOLATE DUMPLINGS

SAUCE:
$^3/_4$ cup brown sugar
$^1/_4$ cup cocoa
1 tablespoon cornstarch

2 tablespoons butter
2 cups water

DUMPLINGS:
1 cup flour
$^1/_2$ cup sugar
2 teaspoons baking powder
1 teaspoon salt
2 tablespoons cocoa

1 egg, beaten
$^1/_3$ cup milk
3 tablespoons melted
    shortening
1 teaspoon vanilla

Combine sauce ingredients in large skillet. Mix well. Heat until sauce comes to a boil and thickens slightly. Remove from heat. Stir dumpling ingredients to blend. Beat one minute. Return skillet to stove. Cover and heat until sauce boils gently. Drop dumplings by table-spoons into sauce. Cover and simmer gently about 20 minutes. Peek just once to see if sauce is simmering. Serve hot with ice cream or whipped topping.

Yield: 6 servings

Family Secret: This was always a favorite with us children at home. Mom sure didn't have to worry about leftovers when she made these!

CINNAMON PUDDING

SYRUP:

1¹/₂ cups cold water
2 tablespoons butter

1¹/₂ cups brown sugar
¹/₄ cup chopped nuts

BATTER:

1 cup sugar
2 cups flour
1 teaspoon baking powder

1 teaspoon cinnamon
2 tablespoons melted butter
1 cup milk

Combine water, butter and sugar. Bring to a boil. Remove from heat and add nuts. Mix together batter ingredients. Pour in a greased 13x9x2 inch pan. Pour syrup over top. Bake at 350 degrees for approximately 35 minutes. Serve warm with ice cream or whipped topping.

Yield: 10-12 servings

CREAMY COOKIE PUDDING

1 pound package chocolate
   sandwich cookies,
   crushed
8 ounces cream cheese,
   softened
1 cup powdered sugar

1¹/₂ cups whipped topping
3 ounce box instant
   chocolate pudding
2 cups milk
Additional whipped topping

Place cookie crumbs in a 9x9x2 inch pan, reserving ¹/₂ cup. Beat together cream cheese, sugar and whipped topping. Spread on cookie crumbs. Beat pudding with milk. Let set for 5 minutes then pour over cream cheese mixture. Top with whipped topping; sprinkle reserved crumbs on top. Chill.

Yield: 8-10 servings

An ounce of enterprise is worth a pound of government aid.

DATE PUDDING

CAKE:

1 cup chopped dates	1 tablespoon butter
1 cup hot water	1 cup flour
1 teaspoon baking soda	1 beaten egg
1 cup sugar	1 cup chopped walnuts

Pour hot water over dates and soda. Let stand until cool. Then add rest of ingredients. Mix well. Spread into a greased 13x9x2 inch pan and bake at 350 degrees for 25-30 minutes. Cool, then cut cake in $^1/_2$ inch cubes.

SAUCE:

2 tablespoons butter	$^1/_4$ cup water
1 cup brown sugar	1 teaspoon vanilla
2 cups water	1 teaspoon maple flavoring
4 tablespoons clear jel	8 ounces whipped topping

In a small saucepan bring butter, sugar and 2 cups water to a boil. Mix well the clear jel and $^1/_4$ cup water. Remove saucepan from heat and slowly stir in the clear jel and water. Return to low heat and cook a while longer, stirring constantly, until mixture begins to look clear. Add vanilla and maple flavoring. Cool. Mix in the whipped topping. In a serving bowl layer the cake cubes and sauce. Garnish with whipped topping and cherries if desired. Refrigerate several hours before serving.

Yield: 10-12 servings

COOKIES 'N CREAM DESSERT

1$^1/_4$ pound package chocolate sandwich cookies, crushed	8 ounces whipped topping
	$^1/_2$ gallon vanilla ice cream, softened

Beat together ice cream and whipped topping. Stir in crushed cookies. Pour in 13x9x2 inch pan and freeze. Let thaw a little bit before serving.

Yield: 12-15 servings

FLUFF PUDDING

2 eggs, separated
$^1/_2$ cup sugar
$^2/_3$ cup milk
1 package unflavored gelatin
$^1/_2$ cup cold water

1 cup whipping cream
1 teaspoon vanilla
3 tablespoons melted butter
3 tablespoons sugar
12 graham crackers, crushed

Beat egg yolks and add sugar and milk. Cook until slightly thickened. Soak gelatin in cold water. Pour hot mixture over softened gelatin. Stir until smooth. Chill until it begins to thicken. Whip cream. Beat egg whites until stiff. Add whipped cream, egg whites and vanilla to chilled mixture. Combine melted butter, sugar and cracker crumbs. Layer crumbs and pudding in clear bowl or pan.

Yield: 6 servings

ORANGE FLUFF PUDDING

PUDDING:
2 egg yolks
$^1/_2$ cup white sugar
$^2/_3$ cup milk
3 ounce box orange gelatin

2 egg whites
8 ounces whipped topping
1 teaspoon vanilla

CRACKER CRUMBS:
13 graham crackers, crushed
   fine

3 tablespoons melted
   margarine
3 tablespoons white sugar

Beat egg yolks; add sugar and milk. Beat together. Heat in double boiler until it thickens slightly. Remove from heat; add gelatin and stir until dissolved. Chill until slightly thickened then add stiffly beaten egg whites, whipped topping and vanilla. Combine cracker crumbs, margarine and sugar. Layer pudding and cracker crumbs in serving bowl.

Yield: 6-8 servings

UPSIDE-DOWN DATE PUDDING

CAKE:

1 cup chopped dates
1 cup boiling water
1/2 cup brown sugar
1/2 cup white sugar
1 egg
2 tablespoons butter

1 1/2 cups flour
1/2 teaspoon baking powder
1 teaspoon baking soda
1 teaspoon salt
1/2 cup chopped nuts

SAUCE:

1 1/2 cups brown sugar
1 tablespoon butter

1 1/2 cups boiling water

TOPPING:

12 ounces whipped topping
2 boxes instant vanilla
    pudding

3 cups milk
Bananas

Combine dates and boiling water; let cool. Blend sugars, egg and butter. Add dry ingredients then stir in date mixture. Pour into a greased 13x9x2 inch pan. Combine sauce ingredients and pour over cake batter. Bake at 350 degrees for 20-25 minutes. Cool. Beat together whipped topping, pudding and milk. Cut cooled cake in small squares and layer cake, bananas and pudding mixture in serving bowl. Chill. Or you can also eliminate the bananas and topping, and just cut the cake in larger pieces, invert on a serving plate and serve warm with whipped topping or ice cream!

Yield: 15-20 servings

The best and most beautiful things in the world cannot be seen or even touched. They must be felt with the heart. - Helen Keller

FROZEN STRAWBERRY DESSERT

CRUST:

1 cup flour
$^1/_2$ cup chopped nuts
$^1/_4$ cup sugar

$^1/_2$ cup margarine, room
   temperature

FILLING:

8 ounces cream cheese,
   softened
$^3/_4$ cup sugar
20 ounce can crushed
   pineapple, drained

1 pint or 10 ounces frozen
   strawberries, slightly
   thawed and chopped
1 large bowl whipped topping

Blend together crust ingredients. Press into a baking pan. Bake at 300 degrees for 5-8 minutes. Let cool a little then crumble crust. Put half of crumbs in bottom of 9x9 inch pan. Combine filling ingredients. Beat until smooth. Pour over crumbs in pan. Sprinkle remaining crumbs on top. Cover and freeze. Let thaw slightly before serving.

Yield: 10-12 servings

Family Secret: This is very handy to serve to guests because it's made ahead of time. Try cutting in squares and garnishing with fresh sliced strawberries and tea leaves.

Marvin & Dorothy Raber

GRAHAM CRACKER PUDDING

$^1/_2$ cup margarine
1 cup brown sugar
$1^1/_2$ cups water
2 rounded tablespoons flour

CRUMBS:
12 graham crackers, crushed
2 tablespoons melted butter

2 rounded tablespoons
   cornstarch
$^1/_2$ cup white sugar
2 egg yolks
1 cup milk

$^1/_4$ cup white sugar
8-12 ounces whipped topping

Melt margarine. Add brown sugar and let come to a boil. Add water and let almost come to a boil again. Combine flour, cornstarch, sugar, egg yolks and milk. Stir into hot mixture. On low heat, stir and cook until it thickens. Cool. Mix cracker crumbs, butter and sugar. Layer crumbs, chilled pudding and whipped topping in a clear bowl. Refrigerate.

Yield: 6-8 servings

Family Secret: Whenever we have a family gathering and Lois asks what to bring we don't hesitate; we tell her to bring her delicious Graham Cracker Pudding!

ICE CREAM PUDDING

50 Ritz crackers, crushed
$^1/_2$ cup margarine, melted
2 3 ounce boxes instant
   butter pecan pudding

3 ounce box instant vanilla
   pudding
2 cups milk
$^1/_2$ gallon vanilla ice cream,
   softened

Mix crushed crackers and margarine. Pat crumbs in a 9x9x2 inch pan and chill. Beat together puddings and milk. Add softened ice cream. Mix well. Pour on crumbs. Chill and serve or freeze, then thaw slightly before serving.

Yield: 10-12 servings

All wise men share one trait in common: the ability to listen.

JIMMY CARTER PUDDING

LAYER #1:
1 cup flour
$^1/_2$ cup margarine, room
  temperature

$^2/_3$ cup chopped salted
  peanuts

LAYER #2:
$^1/_3$ cup peanut butter
1 cup powdered sugar

8 ounces cream cheese,
  softened
1 cup whipped topping

LAYER #3:
3 ounce box instant
  chocolate pudding

3 ounce box instant vanilla
  pudding
$2^3/_4$ cups milk

LAYER #4:
Whipped topping

Chopped peanuts

Mix layer #1 ingredients and press into 13x9x2 inch pan. Bake at 350 degrees for 20 minutes. Cool. Beat together layer #2 ingredients and spread over baked crust. Beat puddings and milk and pour over cream cheese layer. Cover with whipped topping and sprinkle nuts on top. Chill.

Yield: 15-20 servings

MONTANA TAPIOCA

5 cups milk
10 tablespoons pearl tapioca
2 beaten eggs
$1^1/_3$ cups sugar

1 teaspoon salt
1 teaspoon vanilla
8 ounces whipped topping

In saucepan combine milk and tapioca. Simmer for 15 minutes. Do not boil. Stir often. Add eggs, sugar, salt and vanilla and bring to a boil. Remove from heat and set pan in cold water to cool. Stir in whipped topping. Chill.

Yield: 6-8 servings

FRUITY TAPIOCA

6 cups water
$^1/_2$ cup plus 2 tablespoons
    pearl tapioca
3 ounce box strawberry
    jello, or desired flavor

$^1/_2$ cup sugar
Pinch salt
12 ounces whipped topping
Sliced bananas,
    strawberries or pineapple

Bring water to a boil. Add tapioca and cook for 20 minutes or until clear, stirring occasionally. Remove from heat and add jello, sugar and salt. Chill. Fold in whipped topping and fruit.

Yield: 8-10 servings

PINEAPPLE RINGS

1 can sliced pineapple
1 can Eagle Brand milk

8 ounces whipped topping
Maraschino cherries, for
    garnish

In a medium saucepan, place can of Eagle Brand milk, wrapper removed. Cover with water and cook for 2-2$^1/_2$ hours. Check once in a while to make sure can stays covered with water. Add more water if necessary. Cool and refrigerate for at least 12 hours. Drain pineapple. Arrange slices on serving plate. With can opener open both ends of the can of chilled milk. Remove the lid then very carefully push the bottom of the can up until you can slice off a circle to put on the pineapple rings. Put on a dab of whipped topping. Drain cherries and pat dry with a paper towel. Top it off with a cherry!

Yield: 10 pineapple rings

Family Secret: You may want to cook the Eagle Brand milk a few at a time and several weeks in advance as it keeps well in the refrigerator.

LOIS' HOMEMADE ICE CREAM

3 packages unflavored
   gelatin
1^1/$_2$ cups milk
11 cups milk
3^1/$_3$ cups brown sugar, slightly
   packed

Pinch salt
5-7 teaspoons vanilla
1^1/$_2$ pints whipping cream
4 egg yolks
1^1/$_8$ cups white sugar

Soften gelatin in 1^1/$_2$ cups milk. In large kettle scald 11 cups milk. Add gelatin mixture and stir well. Add brown sugar, salt and vanilla. Chill in refrigerator. This can be made a day ahead of time. When ready to freeze whip the cream. Beat in egg yolks and sugar. Stir into chilled mixture. Pour into a 2 gallon can and freeze.

Yield: 2 gallons

MOM'S HOMEMADE ICE CREAM

2 3 ounce boxes instant
   vanilla pudding
2 6 ounce boxes ice cream
   mix

1 can Eagle Brand milk
1 pint cream
1 cup brown sugar
Milk

Beat together all ingredients except milk. Pour in a 1^1/$_2$ gallon freezer can. Add milk to make can ^{3}/$_4$ full. Freeze. This kind does not get icy when you freeze leftovers.

Yield: 1^1/$_2$ gallons

Age may wrinkle your face but lack of enthusiasm wrinkles your soul.

MAPLE NUT PUDDING

1 tablespoon unflavored
   gelatin
$1/2$ cup cold water
$1^1/2$ cups brown sugar
1 cup boiling water
2 cups milk
$1/2$ cup brown sugar

1 tablespoon flour
1 tablespoon cornstarch
2 egg yolks
$1/2$ teaspoon vanilla
Pinch salt
$1^1/2$ cups whipped topping
1 cup chopped nuts, optional

Soak gelatin in cold water. Pour boiling water over sugar. Stir well. Add gelatin. Pour into a flat pan and chill. Cut into cubes. Cook together milk, sugar, flour, cornstarch, egg yolks, vanilla and salt. Cook until thickened, stirring constantly. Cool. Fold in whipped topping, gelatin cubes and nuts. Place in serving bowl and chill.

Yield: 6-8 servings

PINEAPPLE BREEZE

16 ounces whipped topping
20 ounce can crushed
   pineapple, drained
1 can Eagle Brand milk
3 cups miniature
   marshmallows

1 cup cooked rice, optional
$1/4$ cup butter
$1/4$ cup brown sugar
1 cup chopped nuts

Combine whipped topping, pineapple, milk, marshmallows and rice. In a small saucepan melt butter. Add brown sugar and stir until dissolved. Add nuts and toast lightly. Cool, then add to pineapple mixture.

Yield: 10-12 servings

We can only appreciate the miracle of a sunrise if we have waited in darkness.

PRETZEL CHEESECAKE

CRUST:
1¹/₂ cups crushed pretzels
¹/₄ cup melted butter

3 tablespoons brown sugar

FILLING:
8 ounces cream cheese,
    softened

¹/₃ cup sugar
8 ounces whipped topping

TOPPING:
1 can cherry pie filling, or
    other favorite pie filling

Combine crust ingredients and pat into an 8 inch round pan. Bake at 400 degrees for 10 minutes. Cool. Beat together filling ingredients and spread over crust. Top with pie filling. Chill.

Yield: 6-8 servings

PUMPKIN ICE CREAM DESSERT

CRUST:
2 cups graham cracker
    crumbs
¹/₄ cup melted butter

1 tablespoon powdered
    sugar
¹/₂ teaspoon unflavored
    gelatin

FILLING:
³/₄ cup pumpkin
¹/₂ cup sugar
¹/₂ teaspoon salt
¹/₂ teaspoon cinnamon

¹/₄ teaspoon ginger
¹/₄ teaspoon nutmeg
1 quart ice cream

Mix all the crust ingredients together and press into an 8x8 inch pan. Bake at 350 degrees for 20 minutes. Combine all the filling ingredients and mix well. Put on top of cooled crust. Freeze. Top with whipped topping before serving if desired.

Yield: 8 servings

PUMPKIN ROLL

1 cup sugar	1 teaspoon cinnamon
³/₄ cup flour	³/₄ cup chopped nuts
1 teaspoon salt	²/₃ cup pumpkin
1 teaspoon baking soda	3 eggs, beaten

FILLING:

2 teaspoons margarine	1 teaspoon vanilla
8 ounces cream cheese	1 cup powdered sugar

Mix dry ingredients. Add pumpkin and eggs and mix well. Line a cookie sheet with wax paper and spray with cooking spray. Spread mixture on wax paper and bake at 350 degrees for 15 minutes. Invert baked mixture on a clean dish towel that is sprinkled with powdered sugar. Remove wax paper immediately. Roll up cake in towel, starting with long end, and cool completely. Mix filling ingredients. Unroll and spread filling on cooled cake. Roll up again and refrigerate.

Yield: 18-20 slices

REFRESHING ORANGE DESSERT

1 package vanilla instant pudding	3 cups boiling water
1 package instant tapioca pudding	2 11 ounce cans mandarin oranges, drained
3 ounce package orange jello	2 cups whipped topping

Mix dry puddings and jello together. Add boiling water. Stir until dissolved. When cool, add mandarin oranges, reserving a few for garnish. Chill until almost thickened then fold in whipped topping. Garnish with reserved oranges and mint leaves.

Yield: 8-10 servings

RHUBARB CRUNCH

1 cup flour
³/₄ cup quick oats
1 cup brown sugar, packed
¹/₂ cup melted butter or
    margarine
1 teaspoon cinnamon

4 cups diced rhubarb
1 cup white sugar
1 cup water
2 tablespoons cornstarch
1 teaspoon vanilla

Mix flour, oats, brown sugar, butter and cinnamon until crumbly. Press half of crumbs in a greased 11x7x2 inch pan. Cover with diced rhubarb. In a medium saucepan combine rest of ingredients. Cook until thick and clear, stirring constantly. Pour over rhubarb. Top with remaining crumbs. Bake at 350 degrees for 1 hour. Serve warm with whipped topping or ice cream.

Yield: 6-8 servings

STRAWBERRY SHORTCAKE

¹/₂ cup shortening
1¹/₂ cups sugar
2 eggs
1 teaspoon salt

6 teaspoons baking powder
3¹/₄ cups flour
2 cups milk

Mix together in order given. Bake in a greased 13x9x2 inch pan at 350 degrees for 30 minutes or until done. Serve with strawberries and milk or ice cream.

Yield: 18 servings

Do not let your heart be troubled and do not be afraid. John 14:27

TORTE PUDDING

CRUST:
1 cup flour
$^1/_2$ cup chopped nuts
1 tablespoon sugar
$^1/_2$ cup margarine, room temperature

CREAM FILLING:
8 ounces cream cheese, softened
1 cup powdered sugar
$1^1/_2$ cups whipped topping

PUDDING:
3 3 ounce boxes instant vanilla, lemon or butterscotch pudding
$4^1/_2$ cups milk
Additional whipped topping
Chopped nuts or candy bar

Combine crust ingredients and pat in 13x9x2 inch pan. Bake at 350 degrees for 15 minutes. Cool. Beat together cream filling and spread over cooled crust. Beat pudding and milk. Let set for 5 minutes then spread over second layer. Cover with whipped topping and sprinkle nuts or candy on top.

Yield: 15-20 servings

OATMEAL PEACH COBBLER

$1^1/_3$ cups flour
$1^1/_3$ cups quick oats
$^2/_3$ cup brown sugar
$^1/_2$ teaspoon salt
$^1/_2$ teaspoon baking soda
$^1/_2$ cup margarine, melted
1 teaspoon vanilla
1 quart canned peaches
Cinnamon

Combine flour, oats, sugar, salt, baking soda, margarine and vanilla. Mixture will be crumbly. Put peaches, juice and all, in an 11x7x2 inch rectangular pan. Cover with crumbs; sprinkle cinnamon on top. Bake at 375 degrees for 45 minutes. Delicious with ice cream!

Yield: 6-8 servings

Pictured on Reverse Side

The front porch, where the guests spend a lot of time.

Naomi's Nook, one of fifteen guest rooms. Each room is named after members of the family.

HOMEMADE
PIES &
CAKES

HOMEMADE PIES AND CAKES

PIES

CAKES

FROSTINGS

MOM'S FAVORITE PIE CRUST

6 cups flour
$2^1/_2$ cups shortening
1 egg yolk

1 tablespoon sugar
1 teaspoon salt
Water

Cut shortening into flour. Put egg yolk, sugar and salt in a measuring cup and add water to make 1 cup. Mix slightly then add to flour mixture. Mix gently then roll out and put in pans.

Yield: 5-6 crusts

PIE CRUST

2 cups flour
1 teaspoon salt
$^2/_3$ cup shortening, room
    temperature

6 tablespoons cold lemon
    lime soda or water

Mix flour and salt. Cut in shortening. Add liquid and mix lightly until mixture is crumbly. Roll out dough. Place in pans, prick bottom and sides with fork and bake at 375 degrees for 10-15 minutes. Cool and fill with your favorite cream filling. Or fill unbaked crust with a fruit filling (do not prick crust) and bake required time.

Yield: 3 crusts

Family Secret: This crust freezes well, baked or unbaked.

BLACK FOREST PIE

8 ounces whipped topping
9 inch baked pie crust
1 cup milk

$3^1/_2$ ounce box instant
    chocolate pudding
1 cup cherry pie filling

Spread 1 cup whipped topping on bottom of pie crust. Combine milk and pudding. Mix well then fold in $1^1/_2$ cups whipped topping. Spread over whipped topping in crust. Put rest of whipped topping on chocolate layer then spoon pie filling on top. Garnish with chocolate curls. Chill and serve.

Yield: 1 pie

BASIC CREAM PIE

9 inch baked pie crust
2 cups milk, divided
$1/2$ cup sugar
2 tablespoons flour
2 tablespoons cornstarch

$1/2$ teaspoon salt
2 egg yolks
1 tablespoon butter
1 teaspoon vanilla

Scald $1^1/2$ cups milk in top of double boiler. Combine sugar, flour, cornstarch and salt. Stir in remaining $1/2$ cup milk and egg yolks. Stir flour mixture into hot milk and cook until thickened. Remove from heat. Add butter and vanilla. Let cool a little and pour into baked pie crust. Top with whipped topping when ready to serve.

Yield: 1 pie

Family Secret: Here are some variations you may want to try:

Coconut Pie: Add $3/4$ cup coconut to filling when cooled.

Raisin Cream: In small saucepan put $1/2$ cup raisins and cover with water. Bring to a boil then drain. Stir into pie filling while filling is still warm.

Chocolate: Add 2-4 teaspoons cocoa to the thickening of the cream pie recipe.

Peanut Butter: Mix $1/3$ cup peanut butter with $3/4$ cup powdered sugar. Sprinkle on bottom of baked pie crust, saving some of crumbs to put on top. Pour in the cream filling and top with whipped cream. Sprinkle crumbs on top. This can be used with vanilla or chocolate filling.

Technology is wonderful. We have soda cans that last forever and cars that rust out in just a few years.

CREAM CHEESE NUT PIE

2 unbaked 9 inch crusts
8 ounces cream cheese
$^1/_2$ cup sugar
1 egg, beaten

$^1/_2$ teaspoon salt
1 teaspoon vanilla
$1^1/_4$ cups chopped walnuts or
    pecans

TOPPING:
6 eggs
2 cups light corn syrup

$^1/_2$ cup sugar

Cream together cream cheese, sugar, egg, salt and vanilla. Spread on unbaked pie crusts. Sprinkle nuts on cheese mixture. Beat together topping ingredients and pour over nuts. Bake at 375 degrees for 45 minutes.

Yield: 2 pies

Family Secret: Sara Ann entered this pie in the 1991 Charm Days Pie Contest and won first prize with it!

CUSTARD PIE

1 unbaked 9 inch pie crust
$^3/_4$ cup sugar
2 tablespoons brown sugar
2 teaspoons cornstarch
Pinch of salt

2 eggs, separated
1 cup milk
1 cup half and half
1 teaspoon vanilla or maple
    flavoring

Mix sugars, cornstarch and salt. Add egg yolks and a little milk. Stir well. Gradually add rest of milk, half and half and vanilla. Beat egg whites until stiff then fold in. Pour into unbaked pie crust. Bake at 400 degrees for 10 minutes then reduce to 350 degrees and bake 30 minutes longer.

Yield: 1 pie

Family Secret: This is Dad's absolute favorite! And he thinks no one can make custard pies quite as good as Mom! His family agrees with him, too.

CREAMY VANILLA CRUMB PIE

2 9 inch unbaked pie crusts
8 ounces cream cheese
$^1/_2$ cup sugar

1 beaten egg
$^1/_2$ teaspoon salt
1 teaspoon vanilla

FILLING:
2 cups water
1 cup sugar
1 tablespoon flour

1 cup dark corn syrup
1 beaten egg
1 teaspoon vanilla

CRUMB TOPPING:
2 cups flour
$^1/_2$ cup brown sugar
$^1/_2$ cup softened butter or
    margarine

1 teaspoon baking soda
$^1/_2$ teaspoon cream of tartar
$^1/_2$ teaspoon cinnamon

Beat together cream cheese, sugar, egg, salt and vanilla. Spread on pie crusts. In a medium saucepan bring 2 cups water to a boil. Combine sugar, flour, corn syrup and egg. Stir into hot water. Bring to a boil then set aside to cool. Add vanilla. When cooled pour this over cream cheese layer. Mix the topping ingredients until crumbly. Spread over top of pie. Bake at 375 degrees for 30-40 minutes.

Yield: 2 pies

Family Secret: Mom came up with this version of Vanilla Crumb Pie for the 1992 annual Charm Days Pie Contest. It was a winner! She won first prize with it!

CRISPY ICE CREAM PIE

2 cups crispy rice cereal
1 tablespoon melted butter
$^1/_2$ cup marshmallow creme

1 quart softened vanilla ice
    cream

Melt butter and blend with marshmallow creme. Stir in cereal. Press in a 9 inch pie pan. Fill with ice cream and freeze. Serve with fresh strawberries or hot fudge topping.

Yield: 1 pie

EGGNOG PIE

9 inch baked pie crust
1 teaspoon unflavored
   gelatin
1 tablespoon cold water
1 cup milk
$^1/_2$ cup sugar
2 tablespoons cornstarch

$^1/_2$ teaspoon salt
3 beaten egg yolks
1 tablespoon butter
1 tablespoon vanilla
1 cup whipping cream
1$^1/_2$ cups whipped topping

Soak gelatin in cold water. In a medium saucepan scald milk. Combine sugar, cornstarch and salt. Add to milk and cook until thick. Add egg yolks and cook a little longer. Remove from heat. Add butter, vanilla and gelatin. Whip whipping cream and fold into cooled pie filling. Pour in baked pie crust. Refrigerate and put whipped topping on top before serving.

Yield: 1 pie

PINEAPPLE CHESS PIE

1 unbaked pie crust
1 cup brown sugar
$^1/_2$ cup white sugar
1 tablespoon flour
2 eggs, beaten
2 tablespoons milk

1 teaspoon vanilla
$^1/_2$ cup butter
1 cup chopped pecans or
   walnuts
$^1/_2$ cup crushed pineapple,
   well drained

Combine sugars and flour. Add rest of ingredients and mix well. Pour into unbaked pie crust and bake at 350 degrees until top is brown and begins to crack.

Yield: 1 pie

Family Secret: This pie won third place for Sara Ann in the 1993 Charm Days Pie Contest.

It's not a matter of getting old; it's getting old if you don't grow.

PUMPKIN PIE

1 unbaked 9 inch pie crust
³/₄ cup sugar
2 tablespoons brown sugar
2 teaspoons cornstarch
Pinch of salt
¹/₄ teaspoon ground cloves
¹/₄ teaspoon nutmeg

¹/₄ teaspoon cinnamon
2 eggs, separated
¹/₂ cup cooked pumpkin
1 cup milk
1 cup half and half
1 teaspoon vanilla

Mix sugars, cornstarch, salt and spices. Add egg yolks and a little milk. Stir well and add pumpkin. Gradually add rest of milk, half and half and vanilla. Beat egg whites until stiff then fold in. Pour into unbaked pie crust. Bake at 400 degrees for 10 minutes then reduce to 350 degrees and bake 30 minutes longer.

Yield: 1 pie

Abe & Fannie Mast
Charm, Ohio

SOUR CREAM APPLE PIE

CRUST:
1³/₄ cups flour
¹/₄ cup white sugar
1 teaspoon cinnamon
¹/₂ teaspoon salt

¹/₂ cup plus 2 tablespoons
  butter
¹/₄ cup water

FILLING:
6 large apples, peeled and
  chopped
1²/₃ cups sour cream
1 cup sugar

¹/₃ cup flour
1 egg, beaten
2 teaspoons vanilla
¹/₄ teaspoon salt

CRUMBS:
¹/₂ cup chopped walnuts
¹/₂ cup flour
¹/₃ cup white sugar
¹/₃ cup brown sugar

1 teaspoon cinnamon
¹/₂ cup butter
Pinch of salt

Mix crust ingredients and roll out like any crust. (Enough for one 10 inch pie or 2 smaller pies.) Mix together filling ingredients and put into pie shell(s). Bake at 450 degrees for 10 minutes, then at 350 degrees for 30 minutes. Prepare crumbs by combining the ingredients until crumbly. Remove pie from oven and immediately put crumbs on top. Return to oven and bake another 15 minutes until lightly browned.

Yield: 1 or 2 pies

Family Secret: Another Charm Days winner! Sara Ann won third prize with this pie in the 1992 Pie Contest.

The best angle from which to approach any problem is the 'try' angle.

SOUTHERN CHESS PIE

1 unbaked pie crust
1 cup brown sugar
1/2 cup white sugar
1 tablespoon flour
2 beaten eggs

2 tablespoons milk
1 teaspoon vanilla
1/2 cup melted butter
1 cup chopped walnuts or
  pecans

Mix together sugars and flour. Stir in the rest of ingredients. Pour in unbaked pie crust and bake at 375 degrees for 30-40 minutes.

Yield: 1 pie

RHUBARB CRUMB PIE

1 unbaked pie crust

FILLING:
1 cup sugar
2 tablespoons flour
Pinch of salt

1 beaten egg
1 teaspoon vanilla
2 cups diced rhubarb

TOPPING:
3/4 cup flour
1/2 cup brown sugar

1/3 cup soft margarine

Combine all the filling ingredients and pour into pie crust. Mix flour, sugar and margarine until crumbs form. Sprinkle on top. Bake at 400 degrees for 10 minutes then at 350 degrees for another 30 minutes.

Yield: 1 pie

YUMMY CHOCOLATE PIE

1 baked pie crust
7 1.55 ounce milk chocolate
  candy bars

20 large marshmallows
1/2 cup milk
1-2 cups whipped topping

In a medium saucepan heat chocolate bars, marshmallows and milk, stirring constantly, until marshmallows and candy bars have melted. Cool; fold in whipped topping and pour in prepared pie crust.

Yield: 1 pie

EASY CUSTARD PIE

4¹/₂ cups milk
42 large or 4¹/₂ cups miniature
   marshmallows
³/₄ cup white sugar
Pinch of salt
2 teaspoons vanilla

1¹/₂ cups half and half cream
   or 1 can evaporated milk
4 whole eggs, beaten
1 egg white, beaten stiff
2 9 inch unbaked pie crusts

In a large saucepan heat milk until skin forms. Remove from heat and stir in marshmallows until melted. Add sugar, salt and vanilla. Add cream and beaten eggs and egg white. Mix well. Pour into unbaked pie crusts. Bake at 400 degrees for 10 minutes. Reduce temperature to 350 degrees and bake until center is almost set, about 20 minutes.

Yield: 2 pies

DUTCH CHOCOLATE PIE

1 1.55 ounce milk chocolate
   candy bar
¹/₂ cup margarine
2 cups sugar
2 tablespoons cornstarch

3 cups evaporated milk
2 eggs, separated
1 teaspoon vanilla
Pinch of salt
2 unbaked pie crusts

In a large saucepan melt chocolate bar and margarine. Combine sugar, cornstarch, milk, egg yolks, vanilla and salt. Stir into chocolate mixture. Beat egg whites and fold in last. Pour into pie shells. Bake at 450 degrees for 12 minutes then at 350 degrees until almost set. Cool and refrigerate. Delicious with ice cream!

Yield: 2 pies

There is more power in the open hand than in the clenched fist.

ANGEL FOOD CAKE

1 cup cake flour
³/₄ cup sugar
1¹/₂ cups egg whites
    (approximately 12-14
    eggs)

1¹/₂ teaspoons cream of tartar
¹/₄ teaspoon salt
1 teaspoon vanilla
³/₄ cup sugar

Sift together cake flour and ³/₄ cup sugar 3 times and set aside. On high speed beat egg whites, cream of tartar, salt and vanilla. Beat until slightly stiff peaks form. While still beating, slowly add ³/₄ cup sugar. Continue beating until nice and smooth, about 2 minutes. Now remove from mixer and gently, with spatula or wire whisk, stir in dry ingredients. Pour into ungreased tube pan and bake 1 hour at 350 degrees. Place upside down on platter until completely cooled then remove from pan.

Yield: 12-16 servings

Family Secret: This is one of Lois' recipes. We like this real well with Butter Cream Frosting. For a chocolate cake, remove 2 slightly rounded tablespoons flour and replace with that amount of cocoa.

APPLE CAKE

1 can apple pie filling
2 cups sugar
2 eggs
¹/₂ cup vegetable oil
1 teaspoon vanilla

1 teaspoon cinnamon
2 cups flour
1 teaspoon salt
2 teaspoons baking soda
1 cup chopped nuts

Combine ingredients and mix lightly. Pour into a greased 13x9x2 inch pan and bake at 350 degrees for 30-35 minutes.

Yield: 24 pieces

BUTTERSCOTCH CAKE

1 box yellow cake mix
2 eggs

15 ounce can prepared
butterscotch pudding

TOPPING:
1 cup butterscotch morsels
$^1/_3$ cup sugar

$^1/_2$ cup chopped walnuts

Mix dry cake mix, eggs and pudding well. Pour in a greased 13x9x2 inch pan. Combine topping ingredients and sprinkle on top. Bake at 350 degrees for 25-30 minutes.

Yield: 24 servings

CHOCOLATE COLA CAKE

2 cups flour
2 cups sugar
2 tablespoons cocoa
1 cup margarine
1 cup cola
$^1/_2$ cup buttermilk

1 teaspoon vanilla
2 eggs
1 teaspoon baking soda
$^1/_4$ teaspoon salt
$1^1/_2$ cups miniature
marshmallows

Combine flour, sugar and cocoa. Heat margarine and cola to boiling point. Pour over flour mixture then add remaining ingredients in order given. Pour in a greased 13x9x2 inch pan and bake at 350 degrees for 30 minutes. Frost with favorite frosting.

Yield: 24 pieces

Each day is God's gift to you. Make it blossom and grow into a thing of beauty.

CHOCOLATE TWINKIES

CAKE:

1 box chocolate cake mix
1 package instant chocolate
   pudding

4 eggs
$^3/_4$ cup vegetable oil
$^3/_4$ cup water

FILLING:

1 cup shortening
2 cups powdered sugar

2 egg whites, beaten

Combine first five ingredients and mix well. Pour into a wax paper lined jelly roll pan. Bake at 350 degrees for 20-25 minutes. Invert onto wire cooling rack and remove wax paper. Cool. Cream together shortening and sugar thoroughly, then add egg whites. Cut cake in half to make two squares. Spread filling between layers.

Yield: 12-16 pieces

EARTHQUAKE DESSERT

$1^1/_2$ cups coconut
1 cup chopped walnuts
1 box German chocolate
   cake mix

$^1/_2$ cup margarine, softened
2 cups powdered sugar
8 ounces cream cheese,
   room temperature

Grease a 13x9x2 inch pan. (If you use a 13x9x2 inch pan, cake will run over into your oven.) Cover bottom of pan with coconut. Sprinkle chopped nuts over coconut. Prepare cake mix as directed on package. Pour over coconut and nut mixture. Combine margarine, powdered sugar and cream cheese. Stir until smooth. Spoon over cake mix; do not stir. Bake at 350 degrees for 1 hour.

Yield: 24 pieces

*It doesn't help to forgive if you keep recalling that
you forgave.*

GRAHAM STREUSEL CAKE

1 box yellow cake mix
2 cups crushed graham
   crackers
$^3/_4$ cup brown sugar

$^1/_2$ cup butter, softened
$^3/_4$ cup chopped walnuts
1 teaspoon cinnamon

GLAZE:
3 cups powdered sugar
1 tablespoon vegetable oil

Hot water, enough to
   make desired
   consistency

Mix cake mix as directed on box. Combine rest of ingredients. Pour half of cake mix in greased 13x9x2 inch pan. Sprinkle half of crumbs on top. Add remaining cake batter then another layer of crumbs. Bake at 350 degrees for 30-35 minutes. Stir together glaze ingredients. Drizzle over cooled cake.

Yield: 24 pieces

HO-HO CAKE

1 box chocolate cake mix

FILLING:
5 tablespoons flour or 3
   tablespoons cornstarch
1$^1/_4$ cups milk

1 cup sugar
$^1/_2$ cup shortening
$^1/_2$ cup margarine

ICING:
$^1/_2$ cup melted margarine
3 cups powdered sugar
6 tablespoons cocoa

1 teaspoon vanilla
2-4 tablespoons hot water
1 beaten egg

Mix and bake cake mix according to package directions in a jelly roll pan. Cool. Combine flour and milk and cook until thick. Allow to cool. Cream together sugar, shortening and margarine. Beat until fluffy. Beat another 4 minutes into cooled flour and milk mixture. Spread over cake. Combine icing ingredients. Beat until fluffy then spread over filling.

Yield: 24-30 servings

LAZY DAISY CAKE

4 eggs
2 cups sugar
2 teaspoons vanilla
2 cups flour

2 teaspoons baking powder
1 cup milk
6 tablespoons margarine

TOPPING:
10 tablespoons brown sugar
4 tablespoons cream

6 tablespoons melted butter
1 cup coconut

Beat eggs. Add sugar, beating constantly. Add vanilla. Combine flour with baking powder then stir into egg mixture. In saucepan heat milk and margarine. Bring to a boil then add to egg and flour mixture immediately. Pour in a greased 13x9x2 inch pan and bake at 325 degrees for 30-40 minutes. In saucepan mix topping ingredients and heat until sugar is dissolved. Spread on cake as soon as you take it out of oven. Then place under broiler until bubbly. (Not very long.)

Yield: 24 servings

OLD-FASHIONED CRUMB CAKE

2 cups brown sugar
2$\frac{1}{2}$ cups flour
$\frac{1}{2}$ teaspoon salt
$\frac{1}{2}$ teaspoon nutmeg

$\frac{1}{2}$ cup shortening
1 cup sour milk
1 teaspoon baking soda
1 beaten egg

Combine sugar, flour, salt and nutmeg. Cut in shortening. Mix until crumbly. Reserve $\frac{1}{2}$ cup crumbs and set aside for top. To the rest of crumbs add milk, soda and egg. Mix well. Put in a greased 13x9x2 inch pan. Put reserved crumbs on top and bake at 350 degrees for 35 minutes.

Yield: 24 servings

Family Secret: This is one of our favorite cakes not only because it's good, but mainly because Grandma used to make this often. It always brings back some warm childhood memories!

MASHED POTATO CAKE

1 cup margarine, softened
2 cups sugar
2 eggs
1 teaspoon vanilla
1 cup cold, leftover mashed
    potatoes

2 cups flour
$^1/_4$ cup cocoa
1 teaspoon baking soda
1 cup milk
1 cup chopped walnuts

Cream together margarine and sugar. Add eggs, one at a time. Blend in vanilla and potatoes. Combine flour, cocoa and soda. Add to creamed mixture alternately with milk. Stir in nuts. Pour in greased 13x9x2 inch pan. Bake at 350 degrees for 35-40 minutes or until done.

Yield: 24 pieces

LEMON GOLDEN DREAM CAKE

1 box yellow cake mix
3 ounce box lemon instant
    pudding

$^3/_4$ cup vegetable oil
$^3/_4$ cup water
4 eggs

ICING:
2 cups powdered sugar
2 tablespoons melted butter

2 tablespoons water
$^1/_2$ cup lemon juice

Combine cake mix, pudding, oil, water and eggs. Mix well. Pour in a greased 13x9x2 inch pan. Bake at 350 degrees for 30-35 minutes. Meanwhile blend lemon juice, butter and water. Add powdered sugar. Blend well. When cake is done remove from oven and punch holes in it with a fork. Pour icing over hot cake. Cool.

Yield: 18 servings

Family Secret: Cook together 3 cups water, 1 small box strawberry jello and 1 box vanilla tapioca pudding. When cool add 2 cups sliced strawberries. Spoon onto baked, cooled cake and top with whipped topping.

PEANUT BUTTER CANDY CAKE

1³/₄ cups boiling water
1 cup quick oats
¹/₂ cup butter
1 cup brown sugar
1 cup white sugar
1 teaspoon vanilla
2 eggs
1¹/₂ cups flour

1 teaspoon baking soda
¹/₂ teaspoon baking powder
¹/₄ teaspoon cinnamon
¹/₄ teaspoon salt
5 6 ounce size milk
    chocolate covered
    peanut butter cups

Combine water and oats. Cool. Cream butter, sugars and vanilla. Beat in eggs. Blend in oatmeal mixture. Add rest of ingredients except peanut butter cups. Mix well. Pour batter in a greased 13x9x2 inch pan. Chop peanut butter cups and put on top. Bake at 350 degrees for 40-45 minutes.

Yield: 24 servings

PINEAPPLE CAKE

2 cups sugar
2 tablespoons vegetable oil
2 eggs
2¹/₄ cups crushed pineapple
1 teaspoon vanilla

¹/₂ cup chopped walnuts
2¹/₄ cups flour
2 teaspoons baking soda
1 teaspoon salt

Combine sugar, oil, eggs, undrained pineapple and vanilla. Stir in nuts. Sift rest of ingredients. Stir into pineapple mixture. Bake in a greased 13x9x2 inch pan at 350 degrees for 35 minutes. Cool and ice with Cream Cheese Icing. (See Pumpkin Bar recipe.)

Yield: 24 pieces

Very little is needed to make a happy life.

PRALINE CAKE

1 box chocolate cake mix
$^1/_2$ cup butter
$^1/_4$ cup whipping cream

1 cup brown sugar
1$^1/_2$ cups chopped walnuts

TOPPING:
8 ounces whipped topping
$^1/_4$ cup powdered sugar

$^1/_4$ teaspoon vanilla
Chocolate curls for garnish

Prepare cake mix according to package directions. Set aside. In saucepan put butter, whipping cream and sugar. Cook over low heat until butter melts. Pour butter mixture into a greased 13x9x2 inch pan. Sprinkle with walnuts. Pour cake mix batter over top. Bake at 325 degrees for 25-30 minutes. Remove from oven when done and let set for 5 minutes. Invert cake onto a serving tray. Refrigerate until ready to serve. Mix topping ingredients and dab on top before serving. Garnish with chocolate curls.

Yield: 24 pieces

REFRESHING JELLO CAKE

1 box lemon cake mix
3 ounce box lemon jello

$^3/_4$ cup boiling water
$^3/_4$ cup lemon-lime soda

TOPPING:
3 ounce box lemon instant
   pudding

1$^1/_3$ cups milk
1 cup whipped topping

Prepare cake mix and bake in a 13x9x2 inch pan according to package directions. Dissolve jello in hot water. Add soda. As soon as cake is done prick full of holes with fork. Spoon jello over cake. Cool. Mix the pudding and milk well. Blend in whipped topping. Spread over cooled cake and refrigerate.

Yield: 24 servings

Family Secret: For variation use white cake mix, strawberry jello and vanilla pudding.

TURTLE CAKE

1 box chocolate cake mix
14 ounce bag caramels,
   unwrapped
$^1/_2$ cup butter or margarine

7 ounce can Eagle Brand
   milk
6 ounces chopped walnuts
   or pecans
6 ounces chocolate chips

Mix cake mix according to package directions. Pour half of batter in a greased 13x9x2 inch pan. Bake at 350 degrees for 15 minutes. Meanwhile, in double boiler combine caramels, butter and milk. Heat until butter is melted. Cool slightly and pour over half baked cake. Pour on remaining cake batter. Mix the walnuts and chocolate chips and sprinkle on top. Return to oven and bake for 20 more minutes or until toothpick inserted in center comes out clean.

Yield: 24 servings

WATERGATE CAKE

1 box white cake mix
3 ounce box pistachio
   instant pudding mix
1 cup vegetable oil

3 eggs
$^1/_2$ cup chopped walnuts
1 cup lemon-lime soda

ICING:
1 package whipped topping
   mix

3 ounce box pistachio
   instant pudding mix
$1^1/_4$ cups milk

Combine cake mix, pudding mix, oil and eggs. Mix well and add walnuts and soda. Beat 4 minutes. Pour in a greased 13x9x2 inch pan. Bake at 350 degrees for 40-45 minutes. Combine icing ingredients and beat until peaks form. Spread on top of cooled cake and refrigerate until ready to serve.

Yield: 24 servings

Family Secret: This cake has an unusual color but is very good. A good friend of ours, Dottie Butler, shared this recipe with us.

SURPRISE CUPCAKES

1 box chocolate cake mix
8 ounces cream cheese
¹/₃ cup sugar

1 beaten egg
Pinch of salt

Mix cake mix according to package directions. Fill cupcake papers ²/₃ full. Blend rest of ingredients. Drop 1 teaspoon of mixture on top of each cupcake. Bake at 350 degrees for 20 minutes.

Yield: 24 cupcakes

TWINKIES

1 box yellow cake mix
3 ounce box vanilla instant
   pudding

³/₄ cup water
4 eggs
³/₄ cup vegetable oil

FILLING:
1 cup shortening
2 cups powdered sugar

2 egg whites

Mix together cake mix, pudding, water, eggs and oil. Pour in a wax paper lined jelly roll pan. Bake at 350 degrees for 20-25 minutes. Invert onto wire cooling rack and remove wax paper. Mix shortening and powdered sugar thoroughly. Beat egg whites until stiff and add to shortening and powdered sugar. Cut cake in half so you have 2 squares. Spread filling between layers.

Yield: 16 servings

Family Secret: When Carol's around this recipe only serves about 8!

The first step to knowledge is to know that we are ignorant.

WHITE TEXAS SHEET CAKE

CAKE:

1 cup butter or margarine
1 cup water
2 cups flour
2 cups sugar

1 teaspoon salt
1 teaspoon baking soda
2 eggs, beaten
$1/2$ cup sour cream

FROSTING:

$1/2$ cup butter or margarine
$1/4$ cup milk

$4^1/2$ cups powdered sugar

In a large saucepan bring butter and water to a boil. Remove from heat. Combine flour, sugar, salt and baking soda. Stir into the hot mixture. Add eggs and sour cream and stir until smooth. Pour into a greased jelly roll pan. Bake at 375 degrees for 20-22 minutes or until done. Cool for 20 minutes. Meanwhile, for frosting combine butter and milk in saucepan; bring to a boil. Remove from heat; add powdered sugar and mix well. Frost cake and sprinkle with chopped nuts if desired.

Yield: 24-30 pieces

WACKY CAKE

3 cups flour
2 cups sugar
3 tablespoons cocoa
2 teaspoons baking soda
$1/2$ teaspoon salt

$3/4$ cup vegetable oil
2 tablespoons vinegar
1 tablespoon vanilla
2 cups cold water

Combine dry ingredients. Add rest of ingredients and mix well. Pour in a greased 13x9x2 inch pan. Bake at 350 degrees for 25-30 minutes.

Yield: 24 servings

Sin has many tools, but a lie is the handle that fits them all.

CARAMEL CHOCOLATE CAKE

1 package German chocolate
   cake mix
1 cup chocolate chips
14 ounces Eagle Brand milk

10 ounces caramel ice cream
   topping
12 ounces whipped topping
3 toffee candy bars, crushed

Prepare cake mix as directed on package. Pour into a greased and floured 13x9x2 inch pan. Bake at 350 degrees for 10 minutes. Sprinkle with chocolate chips. Continue baking until done. While cake is still warm poke holes about 1 inch apart using handle of wooden spoon. Pour Eagle Brand milk over cake. Let cool. Top with caramel topping then whipped topping. Sprinkle with crushed candy bars.

Yield: 24 pieces

YUM YUM CAKE

1 box white cake mix
2 3 ounce packages vanilla
   instant pudding
8 ounces cream cheese,
   softened

15 ounce can crushed
   pineapple, drained
8 ounces whipped topping
Chopped nuts, if desired

Prepare cake mix as directed on box and bake in a jelly roll pan. Cool. Prepare pudding as directed on package then beat in softened cream cheese. Spread on cooled cake. Spoon pineapple on and top with whipped topping and nuts.

Yield: 24-30 servings

CHOCOLATE ICING

3 tablespoons butter
3 ounces chocolate
3 cups powdered sugar

$^1/_4$ teaspoon salt
$^1/_2$ cup milk
1 teaspoon vanilla

Melt butter and chocolate. Stir in powdered sugar and rest of ingredients. Use for icing cakes or cookies.

Yield: 1$^1/_2$ cups

BUTTER CREAM FROSTING

$^1/_2$ cup butter or margarine,
   softened
4 cups powdered sugar,
   divided

$^1/_3$ cup cream or evaporated
   milk
1 teaspoon vanilla

Cream together butter and half of powdered sugar. Add cream and vanilla. Then add remaining powdered sugar and beat until fluffy.

Yield: enough for 1 cake

CARAMEL ICING

$^1/_2$ cup butter
1 cup brown sugar

$^1/_4$ cup milk
2 cups powdered sugar

Melt butter in a medium saucepan. Add brown sugar and cook over low heat, stirring constantly, about 3-4 minutes. Add milk. Stir until mixture comes to a boil. Remove from heat. Slowly add powdered sugar, beating well after each addition until thick enough to spread.

Yield: enough for a large cake

FAVORITE CHOCOLATE FROSTING

16 ounces ready made milk
   chocolate frosting

8 ounces whipped topping

Beat together 12 ounces of the frosting and all the whipped topping. Spread on cake. In a small bowl melt rest of frosting in microwave. Drizzle over edge of cake. Refrigerate.

Yield: enough for a large cake

Family Secret: This is one kind of frosting that you can really pile on and it's not so rich!

When the outlook is poor, try the uplook.

Pictured on Reverse Side

A selection of cookies.

Horses getting attention from guests at the Inn.

OUR
COOKIE
COLLECTION

OUR COOKIE COLLECTION

APPLE BARS

1²/₃ cups white sugar
1 cup vegetable oil
4 eggs
2 cups all-purpose flour
1 teaspoon baking powder

¹/₂ teaspoon salt
1 teaspoon cinnamon
1 teaspoon baking soda
2 cups chopped apples

Combine white sugar, vegetable oil and eggs. Beat well then add the rest of the ingredients. Bake at 350 degrees in a lightly greased jelly roll pan. Cool and cut into bars.

Yield: 24 bars

Family Secret: These are also delicious with Cream Cheese Icing. (See Pumpkin Bar recipe.)

AUNT MARY'S CHRISTMAS COOKIES

1 cup butter
²/₃ cup sugar
1 beaten egg
1 teaspoon vanilla

2¹/₄ cups flour
¹/₂ teaspoon baking powder
¹/₄ teaspoon salt

Cream butter and sugar. Add egg and vanilla. Combine rest of ingredients and add to creamed mixture. Chill dough. Roll out on lightly floured surface and cut with desired cookie cutters. Bake at 350 degrees for 10-12 minutes or until light brown.

Yield: 2 dozen

HALFWAY BARS

¹/₂ cup shortening
¹/₂ cup butter
¹/₂ cup white sugar
¹/₂ cup brown sugar
1¹/₂ teaspoons baking soda

2 eggs, separated
2 cups flour
1 cup chocolate chips
³/₄ cup brown sugar

Cream shortening, butter and sugars. Add soda and egg yolks. Stir in flour. Pat in 13x9x2 inch pan. Press chocolate chips into mixture. Beat egg whites until stiff. Add ³/₄ cup brown sugar. Spread over chocolate chips. Bake at 325 degrees for 20-25 minutes.

Yield: 24 bars

BROWN SUGAR COOKIES

2 cups margarine
4 cups brown sugar
5 eggs
1 cup milk

1 teaspoon vanilla
6½ cups flour
4 teaspoons baking powder
1 teaspoon baking soda

Cream margarine and sugar. Mix in eggs, milk and vanilla. Combine flour, baking powder and soda. Add to creamed mixture and stir well. Drop on cookie sheet. Bake at 375 degrees for 12-15 minutes. Delicious with Brown Sugar Icing.

Yield: 10-12 dozen

BROWN SUGAR ICING

6 tablespoons butter
6 tablespoons milk

¾ cup brown sugar
2 cups powdered sugar

In medium saucepan combine sugar, butter and milk. Bring to a boil. Remove from heat and gradually add powdered sugar. Spread on cakes or cookies while still a little warm.

Yield: approximately 1½ cups

MOLASSES COOKIES

¾ cup shortening
1 cup brown sugar
1 egg
¼ cup molasses
2¼ cups flour

2 teaspoons baking soda
¼ teaspoon salt
½ teaspoon ground cloves
1 teaspoon ground ginger
1 teaspoon cinnamon

Mix thoroughly shortening, sugar, egg and molasses. Stir in all the dry ingredients. Roll dough in balls the size of large walnuts. Dip tops in white sugar then flatten with the bottom of a cup also dipped in sugar. Bake at 375 degrees until done.

Yield: 4-5 dozen

CHEWY CHEWS

¹/₄ cup brown sugar   1 cup flour
¹/₂ cup margarine

Mix together and press into an ungreased 11x7x2 inch pan. Bake at 350 degrees for 10 minutes. Combine the following:

2 eggs, lightly beaten   ¹/₂ teaspoon baking powder
1¹/₂ cups brown sugar   ¹/₂ cup coconut
2 tablespoons flour   ¹/₂ cup chopped nuts
1 teaspoon vanilla   Pinch of salt

Spread over baked crust. Bake at 350 degrees for 25 minutes. Sprinkle with powdered sugar and cut into small squares when cool.

Yield: 18 squares

CHOCOLATE CHIP MARSHMALLOW BARS

1 cup shortening   1 teaspoon salt
³/₄ cup white sugar   1 teaspoon baking soda
³/₄ cup brown sugar   1 cup chopped nuts
2 eggs   ³/₄ cup chocolate chips
1 teaspoon vanilla   2 cups miniature
2¹/₄ cups flour   marshmallows

In large bowl combine shortening and sugars. Beat until creamy. Beat in eggs and vanilla. Gradually add flour, salt and soda. Stir in nuts, chocolate chips and marshmallows. Spread in a greased jelly roll pan. Bake at 375 degrees for 20 minutes.

Yield: 24 bars

You can often tell what makes a person tick by the way he unwinds.

BUTTERSCOTCH CRUNCH BARS

$^3/_4$ cup margarine
$1^1/_8$ cups sugar
3 eggs
$1^1/_2$ teaspoons vanilla
$1^1/_8$ cups flour
$^1/_2$ teaspoon baking powder
$^1/_4$ teaspoon salt

3 cups miniature
   marshmallows
2 cups peanut butter
1 cup butterscotch chips
1 cup vanilla milk chips
3 cups crispy rice cereal

Cream margarine and sugar. Beat in eggs and vanilla. Stir in flour, baking powder and salt. Spread in a greased 13x9x2 inch pan. Bake at 350 degrees for 15-20 minutes. Sprinkle marshmallows on top and return to oven for 3 more minutes. In saucepan combine peanut butter and butterscotch and vanilla chips. Stir over low heat until melted. Stir in crispy rice cereal. Pour over marshmallows once cake has cooled.

Yield: 24 bars

CHOCOLATE MARSHMALLOW COOKIES

$^1/_2$ cup margarine
1 cup brown sugar
1 egg
1 teaspoon vanilla
$^1/_2$ cup milk
2 cups flour

$^1/_4$ cup cocoa
$^1/_2$ teaspoon baking soda
$^1/_2$ teaspoon salt
Large marshmallows, cut
   in half

CHOCOLATE ICING:
$^1/_3$ cup butter
$^1/_2$ cup brown sugar
2 tablespoons cocoa

$^1/_4$ cup milk
Powdered sugar

Combine margarine, sugar, egg, vanilla and milk. Add dry ingredients. Drop on ungreased cookie sheet. Bake at 375 degrees for 8 minutes. Remove from oven. Top each cookie with a marshmallow half, cut side turned down. Return to oven for 1 minute. Cool. In saucepan combine the icing ingredients except for powdered sugar. Boil until large bubbles form. Cool and add powdered sugar to thicken. Spread icing on top of marshmallow.

Yield: 3-4 dozen

CHOCOLATE CRUNCH BARS

³/₄ cup margarine
1¹/₈ cups sugar
3 eggs
1¹/₂ teaspoons vanilla
1¹/₈ cups flour
3 tablespoons cocoa
¹/₂ teaspoon baking powder

¹/₄ teaspoon salt
3 cups miniature
    marshmallows
2 cups peanut butter
2 cups chocolate chips
3 cups crispy rice cereal

Cream margarine and sugar. Beat in eggs and vanilla. Stir in flour, cocoa, baking powder and salt. Spread in greased 13x9x2 inch pan. Bake at 350 degrees for 15-20 minutes. Sprinkle marshmallows on top and return to oven for 3 more minutes. In saucepan combine peanut butter and chocolate chips. Stir over low heat until melted. Stir in crispy rice cereal. Pour over marshmallows once cake has cooled.

Yield: 24 bars

CHOCOLATE STREUSEL BARS

1³/₄ cups flour
1¹/₂ cups powdered sugar
¹/₂ cup unsweetened cocoa
1 cup cold margarine or
    butter
8 ounces cream cheese,
    softened

1 can Eagle Brand milk
1 egg
2 teaspoons vanilla
1 cup chopped nuts

Preheat oven to 350 degrees. In large bowl combine flour, sugar and cocoa. Cut in butter until crumbly. (Mixture will be dry.) Reserving 2 cups crumb mixture, press remainder firmly in a 13x9x2 inch pan. Bake 15 minutes. In a large bowl beat cream cheese. Gradually beat in Eagle Brand milk until smooth. Add egg and vanilla; mix well. Pour over prepared crust. Combine nuts with reserved crumb mixture and sprinkle over cheese mixture. Bake 25 minutes or until bubbly. Cool and cut into bars.

Yield: 18 bars

CHOCOLATE CHOCOLATE CHIP COOKIES

1 cup brown sugar
1 cup white sugar
1 cup margarine
2 eggs
1 teaspoon vanilla
2 cups flour

1 teaspoon baking soda
1 teaspoon cinnamon
1 tablespoon cocoa
2 cups quick oats
1 cup chocolate chips

Cream sugars and margarine. Add eggs and vanilla. Combine rest of ingredients and add to creamed mixture. Mix well. Drop on greased cookie sheet. Bake at 350 degrees for 8-10 minutes. These are good with icing and chocolate sprinkles to decorate.

Yield: 5 dozen

GRANDMA'S OATMEAL COOKIES

PART 1:
3 cups quick oats
2 cups brown sugar
2 cups flour

1 cup melted butter or
   margarine

PART 2:
2 beaten eggs
5 tablespoons milk

1 tablespoon vinegar
1 teaspoon baking soda

Combine part 1 ingredients. Set aside. Mix part 2 ingredients and stir into part 1. Drop on cookie sheet and bake at 350 degrees for 20 minutes or until done.

Yield: 4 dozen

A lot of people can talk. Saying something is more difficult.

COWBOY BARS

Cream together:

1 cup margarine	1 cup white sugar
1 cup brown sugar	

Add:

2 eggs	$^1/_4$ cup milk
1$^1/_2$ teaspoons vanilla	

Combine:

2 cups flour	$^1/_2$ teaspoon salt
1$^1/_2$ teaspoons baking soda	2 cups quick oats

Add flour mixture to creamed mixture. Mix well then stir in:

1$^1/_2$ cups chocolate chips	1 cup coconut, optional
$^3/_4$ cup chopped nuts	

Spread evenly in a greased jelly roll pan. Bake at 350 degrees for 20-30 minutes. When still slightly warm, drizzle with the following glaze if desired.

GLAZE:

1 cup powdered sugar	A few teaspoons hot water
1 tablespoon vegetable oil	

Cool and cut in bars.

Yield: 24 bars

CORNFLAKE CRUNCHIES

1 cup white sugar	1 cup pretzel sticks, broken
1 cup light corn syrup	up
1 cup peanut butter	1 cup dry roasted peanuts
5 cups cornflakes	

Combine sugar and corn syrup in a large saucepan. Bring to a boil and boil just long enough for sugar to dissolve. (Boiling too long will make cookies hard.) Remove from heat and add peanut butter. Add remaining ingredients and mix well. Immediately drop by spoonful on cookie sheet. (Cookies will set quickly.)

Yield: 4-5 dozen

CREAM CHEESE LEMON BARS

1 package yellow cake mix
2 eggs, divided
1/3 cup vegetable oil

8 ounces cream cheese
1/3 cup sugar
1 tablespoon lemon juice

Mix cake mix with 1 egg and vegetable oil until crumbly. Reserve 1 cup crumbs. Press remaining crumbs in lightly greased jelly roll pan. Bake at 350 degrees for 10 minutes. Meanwhile, beat cream cheese, egg, sugar and lemon juice until light and creamy. Spread on top of cake crust and sprinkle reserved crumbs on top. Return to oven and bake another 12-14 minutes. Cut in small squares when cooled.

Yield: 36 squares

Family Secret: These bars have just a light lemon flavor. They disappear fast when Leon and Lois are around!

DEBBIE COOKIES

1 1/4 cups margarine
3 cups brown sugar
4 eggs
2 teaspoons vanilla
1 teaspoon salt

1 1/2 teaspoons baking powder
2 teaspoons cinnamon
1/2 teaspoon nutmeg
2 cups flour
4 cups quick oats

ICING:
2 eggs, beaten
1 tablespoon vanilla

1 1/4 cups shortening
3 cups powdered sugar

Beat together first four ingredients then add the rest. Drop on cookie sheets and bake in 350 degree oven until set. Do not bake too long or they'll get hard and also don't let these set overnight; bake them as soon as you've mixed them. When cookies are cooled, ice them on the bottom and make sandwich cookies.

Yield: 2 dozen sandwich cookies

EASY CHOCOLATE CHIP COOKIES

²/₃ cup shortening
²/₃ cup butter or margarine
1 cup brown sugar
1 cup white sugar
2 eggs

2 teaspoons vanilla
1 teaspoon salt
1 teaspoon baking soda
3¹/₂ cups flour
1¹/₂ cups chocolate chips

Cream together shortening, butter, sugars, eggs and vanilla. Add salt, soda and flour. Mix in chocolate chips. Bake on ungreased cookie sheet at 350 degrees for 10 minutes.

Yield: 7 dozen cookies

Family Secret: These are Dorothy's favorite kind to make and to eat! A not too hard and not too soft cookie. In other words, they're just right!

EVERYTHING COOKIES

1 cup margarine, softened
1 cup white sugar
1 cup brown sugar
1 egg, beaten
1 teaspoon cream of tartar
1 cup quick oats
1 cup coconut, optional

1 cup vegetable oil
2 teaspoons vanilla
3 cups flour
1 teaspoon salt
1 teaspoon baking soda
1 cup chocolate chips
1 cup crispy rice cereal

Mix in order given. Drop by teaspoonful on ungreased cookie sheet. Bake at 350 degrees until lightly browned. Do not overbake.

Yield: 5 dozen

Family Secret: Time to clean out your cupboards? Try these cookies and add a few of your own ingredients for a different variety!

From the errors of others, a wise man corrects his own.

SOUR CREAM CUTOUT COOKIES

1 cup brown sugar
1 cup white sugar
1 cup margarine
2 eggs
5$^1/_2$ cups flour

1 teaspoon baking powder
2 teaspoons baking soda
1 cup sour cream
1 teaspoon vanilla

Cream sugars and margarine; add eggs and mix well. Sift together dry ingredients and add alternately with sour cream (to which you have added 1 teaspoon vanilla) to the creamed mixture. Chill and then roll out on floured surface and cut with desired cookie cutter. Don't roll dough too thin if you want a thick soft cookie. Bake at 350-375 degrees until set, not brown. Approximately 8 minutes.

Yield: 5 dozen

Family Secret: We like these cutouts anytime of year. Just change cookie cutters with each season or holiday.

PUMPKIN BARS

CAKE:
4 well beaten eggs
1 cup vegetable oil
2 cups cooked pumpkin
2 cups sugar
$^1/_2$ teaspoon salt

1 teaspoon baking soda
2 teaspoons cinnamon
1 teaspoon baking powder
2 cups flour

CREAM CHEESE FROSTING:
8 ounces cream cheese
6 tablespoons butter,
   softened

1 tablespoon milk
1 teaspoon vanilla
3$^1/_2$ cups powdered sugar

Combine cake ingredients. Pour into a greased and floured jelly roll pan. Bake at 350 degrees for 20 minutes. Cream together cream cheese, butter, milk and vanilla. Add powdered sugar. Spread on cooled cake.

Refrigerate and cut in bars.

Yield: 24 bars

Family Secret: These are great with a cup of coffee on a cool autumn evening.

LEMON BARS

CRUST:

1 cup margarine, softened
1/2 cup powdered sugar

2 cups flour

LEMON FILLING:

4 beaten eggs
2 cups sugar
1/2 cup lemon juice

1/4 cup flour
1/2 teaspoon baking powder
Powdered sugar

Mix crust ingredients like pie dough. Then form as a crust in a greased 13x9x2 inch pan. Bake at 350 degrees for 15-20 minutes. Combine filling ingredients. Pour over baked crust. Return to oven and bake for 25 minutes. Cool. Sprinkle with powdered sugar and cut in bars.

Yield: 24 bars

MELTING MOMENTS

1 cup butter
1/3 cup powdered sugar
1 1/4 cups flour

1/2 cup cornstarch
1/2 teaspoon almond extract

FROSTING:

3 tablespoons margarine
2 tablespoons cream

1/4 teaspoon almond flavoring
1 1/2 cups powdered sugar

Preheat oven to 350 degrees. Cream butter and sugar until fluffy. Blend in flour gradually. Add cornstarch and almond extract. Beat at medium speed for 5 minutes until satin smooth. Chill several hours. Roll 1/2 teaspoonfuls into marble sized balls. Bake on ungreased cookie sheet for 12 minutes. Blend together frosting ingredients and spread on cooled cookies.

Yield: 6 dozen

Family Secret: These truly do melt in your mouth!

If you don't want anyone to know it, don't do it.

NO-BAKE COOKIES

1/2 cup margarine
1/2 cup milk
2 cups sugar
1/2 teaspoon salt
3 cups quick oats

6 ounces chocolate chips
1/2 cup coconut, optional
1/2 cup chopped nuts
1 teaspoon vanilla

In saucepan combine margarine, milk, sugar and salt. Bring to a rolling boil. Remove from heat. Stir in rest of ingredients. Press in an 11x7x2 inch pan. Cool and cut in bite size squares.

Yield: 24 squares

Family Secret: These bite size cookies are great for serving with popcorn or other salty snacks.

ORANGE DROP COOKIES

2/3 cup Crisco
3/4 cup sugar
1 egg
1/2 cup orange juice

2 cups flour
1/2 teaspoon baking powder
1/2 teaspoon baking soda
1/2 teaspoon salt

CREAMY ORANGE ICING:
2 tablespoons butter,
    softened

2 tablespoons orange juice
2 cups powdered sugar

Cream Crisco and sugar. Add egg and orange juice. Mix well. Then add dry ingredients. Drop on cookie sheet and bake at 400 degrees for 10-12 minutes. Mix icing ingredients and spread on cooled cookies.

Yield: 4 dozen

Perfection may never be reached but it is worth reaching for.

PEANUT BUTTER DREAM BARS

2 cups quick oats
1¹/₂ cups flour
1 cup chopped nuts
1 cup brown sugar
1 teaspoon baking soda
³/₄ teaspoon salt

1 cup margarine, melted
1 can Eagle Brand milk
¹/₃ cup peanut butter
1 cup chocolate coated
   candies

Combine oats, flour, nuts, sugar, soda and salt. Mix. Add margarine, and mix until dry ingredients are moistened and mixture resembles coarse crumbs. Reserve 1¹/₂ cups and press rest in greased jelly roll pan. Bake at 375 degrees for 10 minutes. Combine milk and peanut butter and pour over crust. Combine candies with the rest of crumbs and put on milk mixture. Bake 20 minutes more on top rack. Cool and cut in bars.

Yield: 24 bars

Family Secret: We like to use seasonal candies for Valentine's Day, Easter and Christmas.

PECAN SQUARES

CRUST:
3 cups flour
¹/₂ cup sugar

1 cup butter or margarine,
   softened
¹/₂ teaspoon salt

FILLING:
4 eggs
1¹/₂ cups light or dark corn
   syrup
1¹/₂ cups sugar

3 tablespoons melted butter
   or margarine
1¹/₂ teaspoons vanilla
2¹/₂ cups chopped pecans

In a large mixing bowl blend together crust ingredients until mixture resembles coarse crumbs. Press firmly and evenly into greased jelly roll pan. Bake at 350 degrees for 20 minutes. Meanwhile in another bowl combine all the filling ingredients except for pecans. Beat well then stir in pecans. Spread evenly over hot crust. Bake at 350 degrees for 25 minutes or until set. Cool and cut in squares.

Yield: 24 squares

RAISIN TREATS

1 cup raisins	1/2 cup liquid (from raisins)
1 1/4 cups boiling water	2 1/2 cups flour
1 cup margarine	1 teaspoon baking soda
1 cup sugar	1/2 teaspoon salt
2 eggs	2 cups quick oats
1 teaspoon vanilla	1 cup chopped walnuts

In saucepan combine raisins and boiling water. Simmer 10 minutes. Drain raisins and reserve liquid. Set aside to cool. Cream margarine and sugar. Mix in eggs, vanilla and liquid. Add flour, soda and salt. Mix in raisins, oats and nuts. Drop on cookie sheet and bake at 350 degrees until done.

Yield: 6 dozen

TEATIME TASSIES

Cream together:

6 ounces cream cheese	1 cup margarine

Cut in:

2 cups flour

Chill. Make balls the size of a walnut. Place each in a greased muffin pan, shaping it like the pan with the thumb. Make a syrup of the following:

1 1/2 cups brown sugar	1 teaspoon vanilla
2 tablespoons margarine, melted	1 1/2 cups chopped nuts
2 eggs	Pinch of salt

Beat eggs into the melted butter. Add sugar, vanilla and salt. Mix in nuts. Pour syrup into each tart. Bake at 350 degrees for 20 minutes.

Yield: 1-1 1/2 dozen

Family Secret: We like to bake these in the real small tart pans. Have patience—they do take time but they are worth the effort!

If we pause to think, we will have cause to thank.

Pictured on Reverse Side

The family room and fireplace downstairs.

Wagon dressed up for the holidays.

SNACK
TIME

SNACK TIME

SNACKS

BEVERAGES

CARAMEL NUT CRUNCH

1/2 cup packed brown sugar	6 cups Cheerios
1/2 cup dark corn syrup	1 cup pecan halves
1/4 cup margarine	1/2 cup slivered almonds
1/2 teaspoon salt	Raisins, optional

Mix together sugar, corn syrup, margarine and salt in a large saucepan. Heat until sugar is dissolved, stirring constantly. Remove from heat and stir in rest of ingredients. Spread in a buttered baking pan. Bake at 325 degrees for 15 minutes. Let cool about 4 minutes then loosen from pan. Then let set an hour until firm. Break into pieces and store in airtight container.

Yield: 8 cups

CEREAL NUGGETS

1 cup packed brown sugar	1/2 teaspoon baking soda
1/2 cup margarine	6 cups Cheerios
1/4 cup light corn syrup	1 cup salted peanuts
1/2 teaspoon salt	1 cup raisins

Heat oven to 250 degrees. Grease two 13x9x2 inch pans. Heat brown sugar, margarine, corn syrup and salt in 2 quart saucepan over medium heat. Stir constantly until bubbly around edges. Cook, uncovered, stirring occasionally, 2 minutes longer. Remove from heat; stir in baking soda until foamy. Pour over Cheerios, peanuts and raisins. Stir until mixture is coated. Spread into pans. Bake 15 minutes. Stir. Let stand just until cool, about 10 minutes. Loosen mixture. Let stand until firm, about 30 minutes. Break into bite size pieces.

Yield: 10 cups

A baby is born with the need to be loved—and never outgrows it!

CHEESE ROLLS

8 ounces cream cheese
1/2 cup sugar
1 egg yolk

18 slices white bread
1 cup melted margarine
1 teaspoon cinnamon

Mix cheese, 1/4 cup sugar and egg yolk together. Cut crusts off bread and roll each slice flat with rolling pin. Spread cheese mixture over slices. Roll up each slice and cut in half. Dip roll in melted margarine then roll in a mixture of cinnamon and remaining sugar. Chill at least 2 hours then bake at 400 degrees for 15 minutes. These can be made ahead of time and frozen until ready to use.

Yield: 36 rolls

CREAM CHEESE MINTS

4 ounces cream cheese,
    room temperature
1-2 drops mint oil

Desired food coloring
2 1/2 cups powdered sugar
Granulated sugar

Combine cream cheese, mint flavoring and food coloring. Work in powdered sugar. Knead with hands. Roll in balls then roll in sugar. Press into desired mold then release. Store in covered containers. These freeze well.

Yield: yield varies depending on what molds you use

CREAMY CHEESE BALL

3 8 ounce packages cream
    cheese
16 ounces Velveeta cheese
2 tablespoons
Worcestershire sauce

1 teaspoon onion salt
1/2 teaspoon seasoned salt
2 teaspoons chopped onion
1 cup shredded Cheddar
    cheese

Cream together cream cheese and Velveeta cheese until well blended. Add rest of ingredients and mix well. Chill, then roll into a ball.

Yield: serves 35-40

CREAMY FRUIT DIP

8 ounces cream cheese, room temperature

7 ounce jar marshmallow creme

Mix together and chill. Serve with a variety of fruits. Hint: Dip apple and banana slices in orange or pineapple juice to keep from turning brown.

Yield: 2 cups dip

CRISPY CARAMEL CORN

7 quarts popped corn
2 cup brown sugar
$^1/_2$ cup light corn syrup
1 teaspoon salt

1 cup butter or margarine
$^1/_2$ teaspoon baking soda
1 teaspoon vanilla
1 teaspoon maple flavoring

In a large saucepan combine sugar, corn syrup, salt and butter. Bring to a boil and boil gently, stirring constantly, for 5 minutes. Remove from heat and add soda, vanilla and maple flavoring. Stir quickly and pour over popped corn in a large mixing bowl. Stir well until popcorn is coated then put in a roaster or cake pans and bake at 250 degrees for 1 hour. Stir occasionally. Cool and break into pieces.

Yield: approximately 30 cups

CRISPY ICE CREAM TOPPING

2 cups crispy rice cereal, slightly crushed
$^1/_2$ cup chopped nuts

$^1/_2$ cup brown sugar
$^1/_3$ cup melted butter or margarine

Mix together cereal and nuts. Brown on cookie sheet in 350 degree oven. Mix sugar and melted butter. Stir into cereal and nuts. Delicious on ice cream!

Yield: 3 cups

CRUNCHY CEREAL SQUARES

2 cups sugar
2 cups light corn syrup
1³/₄ cups butter
2 cups peanut butter

12 cups Cheerios
6 cups crispy rice cereal
4 cups nuts, optional

In a medium saucepan combine first three ingredients. Bring to a boil. Remove from heat and stir in peanut butter. Pour over mixed cereals and nuts. Mix well. Spread in two lightly greased 13x9x2 inch pans. Let set, then cut in squares.

Yield: 48 squares

NACHOS AND CHEESE

2 cans Cheddar cheese soup
1 can nacho cheese soup
¹/₂ can water
1 cup Velveeta cheese

1 pound ground beef,
   browned and drained
Nacho flavored tortilla
   chips

In saucepan combine soups, water and cheese. Stir over medium heat until cheese is melted. Add beef. Serve hot with chips.

Yield: 6-8 cups

NUT ROLL

12 ounce box vanilla
   wafers, crushed
3 cups finely chopped nuts

12 ounce can Eagle Brand
   milk

In a mixing bowl combine all ingredients. Mix well. Divide mixture to make 2 rolls. Roll each one between sheets of waxed paper. Roll out to desired shape and size. Wrap each roll in foil. Chill well. Cut into slices. Store in refrigerator.

Yield: 2 rolls

Good example has twice the value of good advice.

NUTTY APPLE DIP

8 ounces cream cheese,
    room temperature
³/₄ cup brown sugar
1 teaspoon vanilla
Milk or cream to thin

1 cup chopped salted
    peanuts
Red or Golden Delicious
    apples
Orange juice

Blend together all ingredients except last two. Wash and slice apples; dip in orange juice. Drain. Arrange on serving plate and sprinkle some chopped peanuts on top of dip. Refrigerate—if there is any left!

Yield: 2¹/₂ cups

ONION CHEESE BALL

2 8 ounce packages cream
    cheese
3 ounce package cream
    cheese with chives
1 scant tablespoon onion
    powder
6 ounces French onion dip

¹/₄ teaspoon Worcestershire
    sauce
¹/₈ teaspoon garlic powder
1¹/₂ cups shredded Cheddar
    cheese
Chopped nuts

Soften cream cheese. Put all ingredients except nuts into a large mixing bowl and blend together well. Chill then shape into a ball and sprinkle with chopped nuts.

Yield: serves 25-30

PEANUT BUTTER CANDIES

¹/₃ pound graham crackers,
    crushed
¹/₂ pound butter or margarine

1 cup peanut butter
1 pound powdered sugar
2 cups chocolate chips

Combine cracker crumbs, butter, peanut butter and sugar. Work together until smooth. Press this mixture into a 9x9 inch buttered pan. Melt chocolate chips and spread on top. Cool and cut into squares.

Yield: 60 small squares

PINEAPPLE CHEESE BALL

2 8 ounce packages cream
    cheese
2 cups chopped nuts
1/4 cup chopped green
    peppers, optional

1 1/2 teaspoons seasoned salt
2 tablespoons chopped
    onion
8 1/2 ounce can crushed
    pineapple, drained

Mix everything together except nuts. Chill and shape into a ball. Roll into nuts. Refrigerate until ready to serve. Can be frozen.

Yield: serves 20-25

PUPPY CHOW

1 cup chocolate chips
1/4 cup margarine
3/4 cup peanut butter

8 cups Crispix cereal
Powdered sugar

Melt together first three ingredients. Pour over cereal squares and stir until coated. Sprinkle powdered sugar over mixture and stir lightly.

Yield: 8 cups

RANCH SNACK CRACKERS

16 ounces oyster or mini
    snack crackers
1 package dry Ranch
    dressing mix

3/4 teaspoon dill weed
1/4 teaspoon garlic powder
3/4 cup vegetable oil

Combine dressing mix, dill weed, garlic powder and oil. Pour over crackers; mix until all crackers are coated. Spread on cookie sheet and put in 200 degree oven for 15-20 minutes, stirring once or twice. Let cool then store in airtight container.

Yield: 4-5 cups snack

SCRUNCH BARS

1³/₄ cups peanut butter
2 cups powdered sugar
³/₄ cup melted butter or
   margarine

4 cups crispy rice cereal
¹/₂ pound melted chocolate

Mix peanut butter, powdered sugar and melted butter. Stir in cereal. Press into pan, ¹/₂ inch thick, and chill. Cut with a thin, sharp knife and dip in melted chocolate.

Yield: 24 bars

CAPPUCCINO MIX

1 cup dry coffee creamer
1 cup instant chocolate drink
   mix

²/₃ cup instant coffee crystals
¹/₂ cup sugar
¹/₂ teaspoon cinnamon

Combine all and mix well. Store in an airtight container. To prepare add 3 tablespoons mix to 1 cup hot water. Stir well.

Yield: a little over 3 cups dry mix—makes 12 (1 cup) servings

CREAMSICLE PUNCH

2 quarts vanilla ice cream
1 quart orange sherbet
2 quarts milk

1 quart orange soda
1 quart ginger ale

Soften ice cream and sherbet. Use a wire whisk to blend in milk. Stir in soda and ginger ale.

Yield: 50 - 5 ounce servings

If there were no difficulties there would be no triumphs.

HOMEMADE HOT CHOCOLATE MIX

5 cups dry milk
6 ounces dry coffee creamer
1 cup powdered sugar

2 cups dry chocolate drink
mix

Mix all ingredients. Store in an airtight container. Use $1/3$ cup mix to 1 cup hot water.

Yield: 18 - 1 cup servings

Family Secret: Matthew likes his with lots of marshmallows!

PIÑA COLADA PUNCH

$1^1/2$ large cans pineapple juice
(69 ounces)
15 ounces cream of coconut

1 quart vanilla ice cream
2 liter bottle ginger ale

Mix pineapple juice and cream of coconut. With wire whisk or beater blend in softened ice cream. Add ginger ale.

Yield: 30 - ounce servings

PINEAPPLE PUNCH

$1^1/2$ quarts water
48 ounces frozen orange juice
concentrate
48 ounces frozen lemonade
concentrate

46 ounce can pineapple juice
7 cups sugar
4 2 liter bottles lemon lime
soda or ginger ale

Mix everything except soda. When concentrates have thawed, stir, then pour into large container or several small containers and freeze. When ready to use thaw partially and add soda.

Yield: 85 - 8 ounce servings

Worry gives a small thing a big shadow.

Index

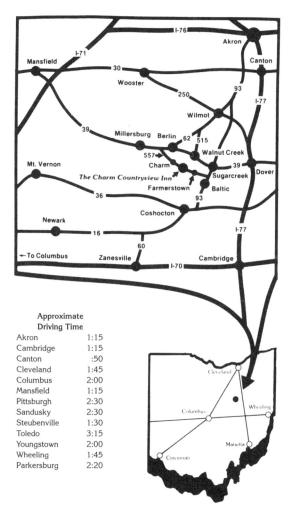

Approximate Driving Time	
Akron	1:15
Cambridge	1:15
Canton	:50
Cleveland	1:45
Columbus	2:00
Mansfield	1:15
Pittsburgh	2:30
Sandusky	2:30
Steubenville	1:30
Toledo	3:15
Youngstown	2:00
Wheeling	1:45
Parkersburg	2:20

From The East

Take I-77 to the Dover exit. Turn West onto Route 39. Follow it to the intersection of Ohio Route 39 and 93 at Sugarcreek. Turn South (Left) on Route 93 and follow it 3 miles till you come to Ohio Route 557. Turn West (Right) onto Route 557 and drive approximately 4$^1/_2$ miles through Farmerstown to the Inn, which is on the left side of the road.

From the West

1$^1/_2$ miles West of Berlin on Ohio Route 39/62 is the turn onto Ohio Route 557. Follow Route 557 through Charm. The Inn is located 2$^1/_2$ miles East of Charm on the right side of Route 557.

THE CHARM COUNTRYVIEW INN
Post Office Box 100
Charm, Ohio 44617
(330) 893-3003
www.charmcountryviewinn.com

Charm Countryview Favorites
Charm Countryview Inn
P. O. Box 100
Charm, Ohio 44617

Please send _____ copies @ $14.95 each $ _____

Postage and handling   @ $ 3.00 each $ _____

Ohio residents add sales tax   @ $ .97 each $ _____

TOTAL $ _____

Name _____

Address _____

City _____ State _____ Zip _____

Make checks payable to Charm Countryview Inn

Charm Countryview Favorites
Charm Countryview Inn
P. O. Box 100
Charm, Ohio 44617

Please send _____ copies @ $14.95 each $ _____

Postage and handling   @ $ 3.00 each $ _____

Ohio residents add sales tax   @ $ .97 each $ _____

TOTAL $ _____

Name _____

Address _____

City _____ State _____ Zip _____

Make checks payable to Charm Countryview Inn

Charm Countryview Favorites
Charm Countryview Inn
P. O. Box 100
Charm, Ohio 44617

Please send _____ copies @ $14.95 each $ _____

Postage and handling   @ $ 3.00 each $ _____

Ohio residents add sales tax   @ $ .97 each $ _____

TOTAL $ _____

Name _____

Address _____

City _____ State _____ Zip _____

Make checks payable to Charm Countryview Inn